HOW HE LOST THE BATTLE BUT WON THE FIGHT

Some Unfortunate Situations Can Be Blessings in Disguise

HOSEA PETERSON

ISBN 979-8-89637-470-1 (paperback)
ISBN 979-8-89637-473-2 (digital)

Christian Faith Publishing
832 Park Avenue
Meadville, PA 16335
www.christianfaithpublishing.com

Printed in the United States of America

ACKNOWLEDGMENTS

First, I want to start off by thanking God for giving my mother, Virginia Peterson, the courage to deal with and raise me. Also, I thank God for giving my mother the courage to raise me as a Black man during the era that I grew up in. Secondly, I want to thank Christian Faith Publishing Company for giving me the platform to allow me to put my memoir and life lessons in a book. Also, I want to thank Lakieda Sanders for initiating this process. I thank my wife, Jasmyn Peterson, for forcing me to stay on course. Lastly, I want to thank my sister, Marion Peterson, for giving me a nephew, Devonte Peterson, who helped me bring the book to fruition in words that I can't explain.

Author's Note

Hope all is well.

Start a new course, reset your expectations, believe in the unseen, be optimistic, never leave your imagination idle, and thrive on identifying, creating, seizing, and maximizing opportunities.

Develop a stronger belief in your dreams, and go for them with undying commitment. You have what it takes to live what you truly desire. Difficulties are meant to raise, not discourage. The human spirit grows strong through conflict. You have a strong mind that can make anything happen as long as you keep yourself centered.

Desire is the starting point of all achievement. Patience and perseverance have a magical effect, before which difficulties disappear and obstacles vanish. You carry a torch that sometimes flickers because the struggle is often dark with despair, but the torch is always bright. Bring out the almighty power within you so that on the stage of life, you can fulfill your destined role.

Success often results after hitting rock bottom or overcoming the biggest hurdle of the journey. Determination, patience, and courage are the only things needed to improve any situation.

Adversity has the power to refocus your priorities, shape your character, unleash your most potent forces, and convert your struggle into fuel. The problems we face can't be solved at the same level they were created.

You have my best wishes for continued progress.

Regards,
HP
5/2/2013

AUTHOR'S NOTE

PREFACE

My goal is that I want this to serve as an inspiration.

I want to inspire people to do something they think they can't do, want to do, or are just ignorant of—the infinite possibilities life has to offer.

It's time for society as a whole to go above and beyond the confines of fear of the unknown, which breeds self-imposed limitations.

I'm encouraging you to embrace adversity and understand the fact that it uplifts the spirit that dwells inside the body, which guides the mind and controls the individual, ultimately building and strengthening character.

Trials and Temptations

> Consider it pure joy, my brothers and sisters, whenever you face trials of many kinds, because you know that the testing of your faith produces perseverance. Let perseverance finish its work so that you may be mature and complete, not lacking anything. If any of you lacks wisdom, you should ask God, who gives generously to all without finding fault, and it will be given to you. But when you ask, you must believe and not doubt, because the one who doubts is like a wave of the sea, blown and tossed by the wind. (James 1:2–6)

It is said that success often results after hitting rock bottom or overcoming the biggest hurdle of the journey.

Determination, patience, and courage are the only things needed to improve any situation.

Adversity has the power to refocus your priorities, hone your character, unleash your most potent forces, and convert your struggle into fuel.

Remember also that all who succeed in life get off to a bad start and pass through many heartbreaking struggles before they "arrive."

The turning point in the lives of those who succeed usually comes at the moment of some crisis through which they are introduced to their "other selves."

*****

HA discovered the genius that slept within his brain after he had met with great misfortune and was confined in a prison cell in Columbus, Ohio.

Being forced through misfortune to become acquainted with his "other self" and to use his imagination, he discovered himself to be a great author instead of a miserable criminal and outcast. Strange and varied are the ways of life, and some are forced to undergo all sorts of punishment before discovering their own brains and their capacity to create useful ideas through imagination.

HK became deaf, dumb, and blind shortly after birth. Despite her greatest misfortune, she has written her name indelibly in the annals of the great. Her entire life serves as evidence that no one is ever defeated until defeat has been accepted as a reality, which one must understand in order to realize that anything is possible.

As you turn through these pages, you will see firsthand how HP, who once was a product of his environment, learned and grew through trial and tribulation—literally. You will see how he was introduced to his better half, his inner being—his "higher self"—and how that person put him on a broad path to realness and an understanding that betterment is for all who strive to apply both the law of the land and the secret law of attraction while bearing principles like integrity as he embarks on this new, profound journey.

Superior Court of the District of Columbia
Criminal Division
United States of America versus HP, Defendant
Criminal Action No. 2011-CF3-8205
Volume 1 of 2
Washington, DC
Wednesday, October 12, 2011

The above-entitled action came on for a jury trial before the Honorable RM, Associate Judge, in courtroom number 312.

This transcript represents the product of an official reporter, engaged by the court, who has personally certified that it represents the testimony and proceedings of the case as recorded.

Appearances:

On behalf of the Government: GP, Esquire, Assistant United States Attorney

On behalf of the Defendant: MM, Esquire, Washington, DC

KG
Official Court Reporter
(202) 879-1072

PROCEEDINGS

THE DEPUTY CLERK: Calling from Your Honor's trial calendar, *United States v. HP*, Case Number 2011-CF3-8205.

GP: Good afternoon, Your Honor. GP for the United States.

MM: MM for HP, who is in the back.

THE COURT: Good afternoon, HP.

THE DEFENDANT: Good afternoon.

THE COURT: What's the last plea offer?

GP: The last plea offer was one count of burglary in the first degree without the armed elements and one count of CPWL. And the Court would not—excuse me, the Government would not have opposed a concurrent sentence.

MM: That was made this morning, Your Honor. And I—and I did communicate that to HP.

THE COURT: Do you need more time to discuss it? I obviously am not involved in the plea discussions, but that's a significant plea offer.

MM: It is. And I would certainly like more time, but it's up to HP. May I have the busher just for a second?

THE COURT: Yeah. I mean, we can. I don't want this opportunity. That plea offer is still open till we call a jury panel. Is that right?

GP: Yes, Your Honor.

THE COURT: You know, it's difficult to talk with the busher. This is what I'm going to suggest, MM. Well, first of all, thank you to the Government for extending that plea offer.

GP: I would like to add one caveat, Your Honor.

THE COURT: Uh-huh.

GP: That—that is a plea offer that I've extended unilaterally. I need to ultimately get approval from my office, but it is on the table as far as I'm concerned.

The Court: Thank you.

MM: HP wanted the opportunity to talk about it before GP went to that trouble.

The Court: Right. No, I appreciate that. I just want to make sure—you know, this is a big decision for you, HP, and the consequences of an incorrect decision are something you want to take the time to look at. What I'm going to suggest is that I give you the lunch hour to talk with your attorney. Have you worked up guidelines and the like?

MM: Yes, Your Honor.

The Court: And as you know, I'm not a judge who goes outside the—is there going to be any request to go outside the guidelines, per se?

GP: No, Your Honor.

The Court: So this is a guideline case, and I just want you to have the full opportunity to discuss it before we get underway.

MM: Very well, Your Honor. It looks like the lunch hour is rolling around anyway.

The Court: So take the time you need to discuss with HP.

MM: Very well, Your Honor.

The Court: And you know my position on accepting responsibility.

MM: I do, Your Honor, as does HP.

The Court: Thank you very much. HP, spend some time with your attorney this—over the luncheon recess, okay? We'll see you back then. Thank you.

GP: Thank you, Your Honor.

The Court: Thank you, GP.

GP: Your Honor, what time should we return?

The Court: It's going to be—well, I'm going to give him a full hour and a half.

GP: Very well.

The Court: This is my thinking. Assuming we'll put the jury office on notice that we may need a panel, and, you know, if we—if we get a panel, it will probably be about 2:30. They release the panels at 2:30, so we're going to have to call for a panel before 2:30 if you want to start it today, and we can get a jury picked and maybe opening statements or something like that.

GP: Very well.

The Court: Is that too optimistic or—

MM: I think it's way optimistic, but I think it's an excellent idea, Your Honor.

The Court: Okay. Maybe I'm misunderstanding what—you mean in terms of picking the jury?

MM: Yes. But I'd be ready for that, Your Honor.

The Court: Right. I—I don't want to have to be ready for that, but if we are ready, we are ready.

MM: But I certainly think it's possible.

The Court: Okay. Well, that's what I'm thinking anyway, and if we have to carry it to tomorrow, we do.

GP: That's fine, Your Honor. Thank you.

(Lunch recess.)

The Deputy Clerk: Calling from Your Honor's trial calendar, *United States v. HP*, Case Number 2011-CF3-8205.

GP: Good afternoon, Your Honor. GP for the United States.

MM: And MM for HP, who is in the back.

The Court: Good afternoon, HP.

MM: Your Honor, I believe we're going to be asking for that jury panel.

The Court: Okay. Could you ask for an extended panel? One through six in the front row, seven through fourteen in the back row.

MM: Is it from left to right, Your Honor?

The Court: Right to left. Fifteen front row, middle to the wall. Thirty-nine front row, right to the wall.

MM: Very well, Your Honor.

The Court: People in the courtroom, we are going to be using all the seats in the courtroom other than the back row on the right, so you can go back there if you wish.

MM: Your Honor asks the questions from the bench of the—of the panel?

THE COURT: Correct.

MM: Do they raise their hand—

THE COURT: Yes. Go around the room and take them in the order in which they come.

MM: Does Your Honor call everyone to the bench or just those who have answered questions, Your Honor?

THE COURT: I usually—it's up to you. I do everybody who answers, obviously.

MM: I would ask if the Court would consider calling everyone up to the bench, Your Honor, because I've certainly had experiences with people who haven't answered a question and—

THE COURT: I said I—I will do what you want. I usually do it that way. If you want to do it differently, I will do it differently.

MM: Oh, I see.

THE COURT: Thank you. How do you want me to describe the case to the jury?

GP: It's a—it's a first-degree burglary while armed. That's the primary charge, Your Honor.

THE COURT: All right. I'm just going to describe it as a burglary, but—

GP: And if I could give the Court the date, time, and location.

THE COURT: Uh-huh.

GP: It occurred on April 27, 2011.

THE COURT: Uh-huh.

GP: At approximately 1:28 p.m. The address is 1435 Good Hope Road, Southeast, Washington, DC.

THE COURT: Anything else you want me to say about the case?

GP: No, Your Honor.

THE COURT: You just want to describe it as a burglary at that—

GP: Actually, it was a burglary and shooting, discharge of a weapon.

THE COURT: Nobody injured?

GP: Nobody injured.

THE COURT: How long is the case going to last?

GP: I'd say the Government's case would take no longer than a day and a half, if that.

The Court: So it will be to them on Tuesday. You can be seated, sir. I take it, MM, you don't want any additional time, right?

MM: That is correct, Your Honor.

The Court: Okay. We believe it will be fifteen-year similar offenses, which I would do burglary, robbery, or firearms, serious assaults.

MM: Um-hmmm.

The Court: Now, at the end of questioning, if I say, "Does Counsel have additional questions?" that means I'm prepared to seat the juror. If I indicate "Counsel" or "I don't have additional questions," I'm prepared to excuse the juror. So if you want to step in at that point, that's fine. Otherwise, people will go. Once we get thirty-six, we'll go. Do your strikes at the bench; alternate Government, defense. We'll move jurors after two rounds, every two rounds: pass, pass, terminate.

MM: Two for the defense, two for the Government, Your Honor, or—

The Court: We have to alternate under the case law: one, one.

MM: I see.

The Court: So it will be one, one, one, one, move, and then one, one, one, one, move.

MM: Very well.

The Court: Pass, pass, terminate the jury selection. Anything else you want me to ask about?

GP: No, Your Honor.

The Court: In general, just the standard?

GP: Yeah. Well, actually, there might be. I would ask the Court to consider the fact that the complaining witness—we actually have two complaining witnesses, one of whom will be coming in from the back. He's in DC Jail now. We will have DC—

The Court: I can do that at the time. I'm not going to void the other panel.

GP: That's fine. I just wanted to propose it.

The Court: So you want me to describe it as a burglary at the address. It was a discharge of a weapon, but nobody was injured?

GP: That's correct.

The Court: Okay. If you could just go over—sir, if you could go over—I apologize, put you all three together, but—

Unidentified Speaker: We're all family members.

The Court: Okay. Great.

MM: May I have a moment to address a witness issue, Your Honor?

The Court: Um-hmmm. I don't sit on Fridays, so it will be today, tomorrow, Monday.

GP: Very good.

MM: When appropriate, Your Honor, there is one or two preliminary issues I'd like to address with the Court.

The Court: Sure.

MM: Having to do with evidence that was—it was numerous objects that were allegedly found as part of a search of my client's house, some of which the Government has told me they don't intend to introduce. Some of it might have been prejudicial. But I think we resolved, like, 95 percent of our issues. I just want to put it on the record. There was a handwritten letter that the Government tells me they do not intend to introduce. There was a picture of four individuals; none of them were the defendant, but the Government says they don't intend to introduce a watch, and my client's videotaped statement, which the Government tells me they do not intend to introduce in their case in chief, but, of course, would reserve to use in rebuttal if the defendant testifies.

There was an envelope that was addressed to HP, which has "FCI" as part of the address, and the Government has agreed to redact the FCI portion of that envelope. And there is one issue we were not able to resolve. There was some forensics found at the crime scene, also allegedly an unspent cartridge found at HP's place. The Government does not know whether that cartridge is of the same caliber as the forensics found at the crime scene. It was indicated to me that if it is not, they don't intend to introduce it, and we're hoping to find that out by the morning.

GP: Those representations are correct, Your Honor.

THE COURT: Thank you very much. How many witnesses in this case?

GP: I'm sorry, Your Honor?

THE COURT: Witnesses—number?

GP: No more than twelve, Your Honor.

THE COURT: How many long? How many short?

GP: Four are long; the rest are relatively short, if not very short.

THE COURT: And I thank you. Okay.

(Prospective jury panel sworn.)

THE COURT: Anybody have any difficulty hearing me at this time?

JURY PANEL: No.

THE COURT: Okay. Ladies and gentlemen, you've been called for potential service in a criminal case. It's *United States v. HP*. He is charged—I'm summarizing the charges essentially—with a burglary that occurred on April 27, 2011, alleged to have occurred.

During the course of the burglary, a weapon was discharged, but nobody was injured. And so, he has charges associated with that event. He's entered a plea of not guilty, denying the charges, so as a result, we'll have a jury trial.

The way jury selection will work is I'm going to ask a series of questions. If you have an affirmative answer to any one of the questions, please raise your hand and give us the last three numbers of your juror number. We do not need your name or your answer at that time, just the last three numbers of your juror number. I'll take the numbers in the order in which you arrived in the courtroom, which is in the jury box first on my left, front to back, and then on my right, front to back.

We obviously have a computer list. We have to keep you in the exact order that you appear on the list, or you'll be here for a long time. There are no right or wrong answers to the questions. If you think the question applies to you, just raise your hand and give us your number. Even if you have a question about the question, raise your hand and give us your number because, at the end, I'm going to speak very briefly to all of you under a busher. So that's why we do not need your answers in open court.

The first thing we're going to do is have the parties introduce themselves and potential witnesses in the case. We want to know whether anybody knows the lawyers or the witnesses involved in the case.

GP: Thank you, Your Honor. Good afternoon, ladies and gentlemen.

Jury Panel: Good afternoon.

GP: My name is GP. I'm the assistant United States attorney here in the city of Washington, DC. It's a pleasure to make your acquaintance.

The United States anticipates calling some or all of the following individuals: Maria Beckham, Maurice Beckham, Diamond Johnson, Joseph Harris; Metropolitan Police Officers Chelsea Pulaski, Ryan Savoy, Todd Korsen; MPD Detective Justin Bolding; crime scene search officers Erin Price and Timothy Ignas; and MPD Detectives Rodney Hollins and Timothy Francis. Thank you, ladies and gentlemen.

The Court: Do you know GP or any of the witnesses announced by him?

(No affirmative response.)

The Court: That statement is made for the court reporter, ladies and gentlemen. MM?

MM: Thank you, Your Honor.

Good afternoon, ladies and gentlemen. My name is MM. I'm a criminal defense attorney here in Washington, DC, and I represent the defendant in this case, HP. HP, if I could just ask you to stand up and face the jury for a second and then have a seat. Thank you, sir.

During the course of this case, you may hear testimony from witnesses, or you may hear about the following witnesses: SC, FP, DH, VP, DV, and JH. Thank you.

The Court: Anybody know MM, HP, or any of the witnesses announced by MM?

(No affirmative response.)

The Court: Ladies and gentlemen, it's alleged this event occurred at or near 1435 Good Hope Road, Southeast. That's 1435 Good

Hope Road, Southeast. Does anybody live or work in that immediate area?

(Juror raises hand.)

Your number, sir?

THE JUROR: 257.

THE COURT: Number 1, 257.

(Another juror raises his hand.)

THE COURT: Your number?

THE JUROR: 331.

THE COURT: 331, that's Number 18. Anybody else?

THE JUROR: 391.

THE COURT: I'm sorry. Could you raise your hand?

THE JUROR: 391.

THE COURT: Okay. Thank you, sir. 391, Number 60.

Ladies and gentlemen, has any member of the panel or a close family member ever worked for any law enforcement agency, including the Metropolitan Police Department, or do you have an application pending to work at such an agency? That's you or a family member—ever worked for a law enforcement agency, including MPD—or do you have an application pending at this moment?

(Juror raises her hand.)

THE COURT: Your number, ma'am?

THE JUROR: 032.

THE COURT: 032, Number 3. 257, Number 1. Yes, ma'am?

THE JUROR: 423.

THE COURT: 423, Number 13, back row on the left.

THE JUROR: 202.

THE COURT: Thank you. 202, Number 36.

THE JUROR: 368.

THE COURT: 368, Number 35. On my right, front row.

THE JUROR: 605.

THE COURT: 605, Number 40.

THE JUROR: 054.

THE COURT: 054, Number 39. Anybody else? Okay. Back row.

THE JUROR: 630.

THE COURT: 630, Number 59. Let me know if I'm going too fast. Everybody caught up?

Okay. Ladies and gentlemen, has any member of the panel ever been a lawyer involved in criminal law, either for the prosecution or defense, at any point in your career?

Your number, ma'am?

THE JUROR: 423.

THE COURT: 423, Number 13.

THE JUROR: 262.

THE COURT: 262, Number 37.

Ladies and gentlemen, obviously there will be some police officers who testify for the Government. At the end of the case, the Court will instruct the jury that you have to evaluate a police officer's testimony like you do any other witness—that you can't give more weight or less weight to the testimony of a police officer merely because he or she is a police officer. You have to listen to their testimony and decide whether they're credible.

Does any member of the panel have any difficulty following that principle of law, or would tend to believe or disbelieve police officers solely because they are police officers?

Your number?

THE JUROR: 889.

THE COURT: 889, Number 51. Yes.

THE JUROR: 057.

THE COURT: 057, Number 52.

Ladies and gentlemen, also at the end of the case, the Court will instruct the jury that HP, as he sits there, is an innocent person because he's merely a person charged in a criminal case. And like anybody charged in a criminal case, he's presumed to be innocent, and it's the Government's burden to prove him guilty; that under our system of justice, no person is required to prove themselves innocent, but it is the Government's job to prove them guilty.

Does any member of the panel have any difficulty following that principle of law or would require HP to prove himself innocent?

(No affirmative response.)

Ladies and gentlemen, I have a multipart question now. It has several parts to it, and I'm going to repeat it. So please do not raise your hand until the end, when I ask for all the hands. And that is, in the last fifteen years, has any member of the panel or a close family member been a victim of, a witness to, or arrested for crimes similar to the one charged here, which is a burglary, attempted robbery, an assault, or something like that?

Let me repeat it. Has any member of the panel or a close family member within the last fifteen years been a victim of, witness to, or arrested for any violent offense, including burglary, robbery, assault, or offenses like that? If any member of the panel or a close family member meets that criterion, please raise your hand at this time.

Your number, sir?

THE JUROR: 420.

THE COURT: 420, Number 7.

THE JUROR: 688.

THE COURT: 688, Number 7. On my left?

THE JUROR: 506.

THE COURT: 506, Number 15.

THE JUROR: 512.

THE COURT: 512, Number 20. Next row, please?

THE JUROR: 584.

THE COURT: 584, Number 21. Next row, please.

THE JUROR: 778.

THE COURT: 778, Number 28. Next row, please.

THE JUROR: 202.

THE COURT: I'm sorry?

THE JUROR: 202.

THE COURT: Thank you very much. 202, Number 36.

THE JUROR: 368.

THE COURT: 368, Number 35.

THE JUROR: 114.

THE COURT: 114, Number 33. On my right, front row?

THE JUROR: 054.

THE COURT: 054, Number 39. Next row, please? Anybody in the next row?

THE JUROR: 914.

THE COURT: I'm sorry. Was there somebody in the front row? Oh, thank you, ma'am. 914, Number 50.

THE JUROR: 799.

THE COURT: 799, Number 47.

THE JUROR: 845.

THE COURT: 845, Number 46. Next row? Oh, I'm sorry.

THE JUROR: 258.

THE COURT: 258, Number 49. Next row, please.

THE JUROR: 057.

THE COURT: 057, Number 52.

THE JUROR: 563.

THE COURT: 563, Number 56. Last row?

THE JUROR: 391.

THE COURT: Okay. Who said 891?

THE JUROR: 391.

THE COURT: 391, Number 60.

THE JUROR: 808.

THE COURT: 808, Number 57. Any member of the panel have any difficulty being fair and impartial to either side merely because of the nature of the charge itself?

Your number?

THE JUROR: 506.

THE COURT: Number 15, 506. Any member of the panel, because of religious, philosophical, or moral beliefs, is unable to sit in judgment of another person?

THE JUROR: 391.

THE COURT: 391, that's Number 60.

THE JUROR: 507.

THE COURT: Okay. Hold on one second. I've got to see where you're sitting. Where was 507?

Thank you. That's 057, right?

THE JUROR: Yes.

THE COURT: Thank you. Number 52.

Ladies and gentlemen, let's talk about the length of the case. Trial is a human endeavor. It involves human beings, and our lawyers are sometimes questioning witnesses for the first time. We can give you an estimate as to how long the evidence will last. This will be a relatively short case. It doesn't mean it's not an important case to the parties; it's just that the evidence may not take as long as you might expect. Okay, so the Court does not sit with jury trials on Friday, so Friday is off because we have too many other cases in the courthouse and we can't get to jury trials. So we—what's today? Wednesday, yeah.

MM: Yes, Your Honor.

The Court: Tomorrow is Thursday. We'll be in trial Monday, Thursday, and Monday. The case will either be over late Monday or early Tuesday. That's our best estimate right now. So it's tomorrow, Monday, and Tuesday. That's how long we expect the evidence to last. Now, that's assuming everybody shows up on time, no juror gets sick, nobody has an emergency, we don't have a fire drill, and we don't have a bomb scare. You know, stuff happens.

And that's how long we expect the evidence to last. I can't tell you how long a jury will deliberate. That's up to the jury. We can just estimate the evidence. Now, we appreciate everybody being here, but as you know, you're required by law to be here. You may have read in the paper that the chief judge has been issuing arrest warrants for jurors who did not show up after being summoned, because you're required by law to be here. It's a criminal offense not to offer yourself for jury service. And you cannot—well, you do not suffice in offering yourself for jury service by coming down to the court and saying, "I'm too busy to serve." Everybody has an important job. No job is more important than another. We have jurors who come down and forgo hourly wages to sit on juries. So generally, your job is not a hardship.

I am going to ask a hardship question. Please understand it's up to the Court to determine whether it's a real hardship. But if you weren't willing to sit on a case of this length, then you weren't willing to fulfill your obligation for jury service. Your summons says you should keep at least one week clear for potential service. This will obviously be a lot shorter than that. So if I do entertain your hardship request and I grant it, you're going to be ordered to go back to the jury office to pick a new date to come back to jury service when your calendar is clear, just so that we all understand that.

With that in mind, based on the estimate we've given you, is any member of the panel, because of personal, professional, or other hardships, unable to sit to the conclusion of the case?

Your number, ma'am?

THE JUROR: 032.

THE COURT: 032, Number 3. On the left?

THE JUROR: 584.

THE COURT: 584, Number 21. Yes, ma'am, in the box?

THE JUROR: 705.

THE COURT: 705, Number 12. Front row, yes, ma'am?

THE JUROR: 152.

THE COURT: 152, Number 6. On my left, front row?

THE JUROR: 360.

THE COURT: 360, Number 43. Next row?

THE JUROR: 914.

THE COURT: 914, Number 50.

THE JUROR: 799.

THE COURT: 799, Number 47.

THE JUROR: 845.

THE COURT: 845, Number 46.

Okay. Sometimes people roll the dice on that question, which is fine with me. You can roll the dice if you want. But in the end, if you end up in the box and raise your hand, and you just remembered somewhere you had to go, you'll be—you'll be enjoying our company while you're serving on the jury.

Everybody had enough time?

Okay. Ladies and gentlemen, I'm going to ask one last question. Does any member of the panel wish to bring anything to my attention or to the parties' attention that you think affects your ability to be fair and impartial that we haven't otherwise asked you about?

THE COURT: Okay, ladies and gentlemen, I'm going to begin the individual questioning. I'm going to call two numbers. The first can come right to the bench; the second number, there's a seat at the end of the railing there. You can take that seat.

Now, I'm basically going to go in the jury box, on my left, front to back, and my right, front to back. So if the person next to you gets up and comes to the seat, that means you're next. Feel free to run to the restroom or—and come right back. But we can't have you in the hallway because we need you in the courtroom. As soon as I have enough jurors qualified, we're going to begin jury selection. The only exception I'll make to that is for those people who are requesting a hardship; you might as well go out and make alternative arrangements because you're not all going to be excused. So you can start making calls to let people know you may be on a jury and tied up. So I'll let you go out and make that call. Other than that, there's no sense in talking about it.

Can I have Juror 257 first and 174 next. Juror 174, if you can take that seat there.

(Bench conference.)

THE COURT: Right up here, sir. Right up here, sir. This is Juror 257. Sir, you indicated you might live or work near the area?

THE JUROR: Yeah. I—I live on Minnesota Avenue. I want to bring this up because I'm over in that area a lot. But when I walked in here, I looked at the alleged person, and he—

THE COURT: No. It is a person. He's alleged to have—

THE JUROR: Well, it is a person, but I mean he's alleged—

THE COURT: Alleged to have done—

THE JUROR: To have done something. And I kept looking, like I may have known him. I don't know him personally, but I may have seen him somewhere. But that's—you know, I just wanted to bring that up.

THE COURT: Well, do you think that's going to affect your ability—

THE JUROR: Oh, no. No. No, that wouldn't affect—

THE COURT: You don't have any specific memory of interactions with him?

THE JUROR: Oh, no. None whatsoever.

THE COURT: No bad experience?

THE JUROR: No. No. Nothing like that, uh-uh.

THE COURT: You also indicated either you or someone you knew was associated with law enforcement.

THE JUROR: Yes, my nephew.

THE COURT: What does he do?

THE JUROR: Well, he's—well, he's just become a lawyer. He was with the DEA. He just left the DEA.

THE COURT: Well, first of all, congratulations to your nephew.

THE JUROR: Oh, thank you.

THE COURT: And so he was in drug crimes?

THE JUROR: Yeah.

THE COURT: Okay.

THE JUROR: Yeah.

THE COURT: We don't have any indication that this was—

THE JUROR: Yeah. Drug-related. I was just bringing that up.

THE COURT: So did any other question apply to you?

THE JUROR: No. That was—I—I have one question I wanted to present to you.

THE COURT: Yes?

THE JUROR: It has nothing to do with this, just me personally, because of my condition. I have prostate—

THE COURT: Uh-huh.

THE JUROR: And a lot of times, I have to run now—

THE COURT: You just—if we're in trial, you just raise your hand, we'll take a recess and—

THE JUROR: Because, you know, when I saw that my vice president served on a jury, I knew I could come down and serve.

THE COURT: Thank you so much.

THE JUROR: So—

THE COURT: Anything else—

THE JUROR: But other than that—

THE COURT: Anything that would affect your ability to be fair and impartial?

THE JUROR: None whatsoever.

THE COURT: Could you be fair to HP?

THE JUROR: Sure.

THE COURT: And could you be fair to the Government?

THE JUROR: Yes, by all means.

THE COURT: Okay. Any questions?

THE JUROR: No.

THE COURT: Thank you. You can be seated.

THE JUROR: Thank you.

THE COURT: 174. 032 next. Yeah, that's you. You didn't answer any questions. Did any questions apply to you?

THE JUROR: No, sir.

THE COURT: Okay. Anything affect your ability to be fair and impartial to either side?

THE JUROR: No, sir.

THE COURT: Any questions?

GP: No questions.

THE COURT: Thank you. You can be seated. 032. 619 next. Yes, ma'am. You indicated you might have a hardship?

THE JUROR: Yes. My daughter has a seizure disorder.

THE COURT: I'm sorry?

THE JUROR: My daughter has a seizure disorder, and I have someone sitting with her tomorrow, but I need to make arrangements to have someone with her.

THE COURT: I don't have any questions.

GP: No questions.

MM: No, Your Honor.

THE COURT: Ma'am, you can go back to the jury room. Thank you. 619. 988 next. Yes, sir. You didn't answer any questions. Did any questions apply to you?

THE JUROR: No, I don't think so.

THE COURT: Anything that you know of affecting your ability to be fair and impartial to either side?

THE JUROR: I don't think so.

The Court: Any questions?

GP: No.

The Court: You can be seated, sir. Thank you. 988. 152 next.

Yes, ma'am. You didn't answer any questions. Did any questions apply to you?

The Juror: No.

The Court: Anything you can think of that affects your ability to be fair and impartial to either side?

The Juror: No.

The Court: Any questions?

Thank you. You can be seated now. 152. 420 next. Hi. You indicated you may have a hardship?

The Juror: Yeah. Well, my daughter is on crutches, and she—her—we live near campus with the school, and she's—I always—I'm a stay-at-home mom, so I drive her back and forth a lot—from one part to the other. And I'm just knowing that if it's three or four days, I'm going to be very worried.

The Court: Okay. I'm not sure that's going to be a hardship—

The Juror: That's fine. Fine.

The Court: You didn't answer any other questions. Did any questions—

The Juror: No, the others are fine.

The Court: Okay. Could you be fair to both sides in this case?

(Juror nods.)

The Court: Thank you, ma'am. You can be seated. I'll reserve 420. And 730 next. Ma'am, you're next. You indicated either you or someone you knew had an experience with a similar offense?

The Juror: Yes. Well, quasi similar.

The Court: Okay.

The Juror: Since I—it was a dare—twice went in, I guess, drive-by shootings where I had to testify in the grand jury. And then once I had my house broken into while I was there.

The Court: Okay. And first of all, with regard to these events, when did they occur?

The Juror: They were roughly five years ago, five or six years ago.

THE COURT: And did you—you were a witness in the grand jury. Was anybody arrested?

THE JUROR: They arrested. I did testify to the grand jury, but I don't know what happened. I don't know if they settled it. It didn't—it didn't go farther than that for me. And then on the other—when my house was broken into, the police weren't able to catch them.

THE COURT: I'm sorry? The police—

THE JUROR: Were not able to catch them.

THE COURT: And when did that occur?

THE JUROR: That was roughly—that was also, like, seven years ago.

THE COURT: And that was in the District of Columbia?

THE JUROR: Both of those were, yeah.

THE COURT: Okay. Any of those experiences affect your ability to be fair and impartial in this case?

THE JUROR: I don't think so.

THE COURT: They wouldn't?

THE JUROR: No, they won't.

THE COURT: Okay. When you say "I don't think so," sometimes that means—

THE JUROR: Oh. No, they won't.

THE COURT: They won't. Okay. You can be fair to HP?

THE JUROR: Yep.

THE COURT: Can you be fair to the Government?

THE JUROR: I think so, yes.

THE COURT: Okay. Any questions?

THE JUROR: No.

THE COURT: Thank you. You can be seated. 730. 105 next. Hi. How are you? Don't worry. Don't worry.

THE JUROR: I thought you were just questioning the ones who raised their hands.

THE COURT: Yeah. No. We're trying to talk to everybody.

THE JUROR: Okay.

THE COURT: You didn't answer any questions. Did any questions apply to you?

THE JUROR: No.

THE COURT: Can you think of anything that affects your ability to be fair and impartial, either to the defense or the Government?

THE JUROR: No.

THE COURT: Any questions?

MM: No.

THE COURT: Thank you. You can be seated. 150. 688 next. Yeah, right up here, sir. Hi. How are you? We're talking to everybody. You did not answer any questions. Did any questions apply to you?

THE JUROR: Not that I could think of, no.

THE COURT: Okay. Anything affect your ability to be fair and impartial to HP or the Government in this case?

THE JUROR: No.

THE COURT: Any questions?

THE JUROR: No.

THE COURT: Thank you. You can be seated. 688. 103 next. Yes, right up here. You indicated either you or somebody you knew had an experience with a similar offense?

THE JUROR: I was assaulted in Georgetown four years ago by a mentally ill man off his medication.

THE COURT: Okay. Was anybody arrested in connection with that?

THE JUROR: They decided not to prosecute if he took his medication.

THE COURT: Okay. Anything affect your ability to be fair and impartial arising from that?

THE JUROR: No.

THE COURT: Can you keep it separate and apart from the evidence you hear in this case?

THE JUROR: Yes.

THE COURT: Can you be fair to HP?

THE JUROR: Yes.

THE COURT: Can you be fair to the Government?

THE JUROR: Yes.

THE COURT: Any questions?

THE JUROR: No.

THE COURT: Sir, you can be seated. 103. 705 next. Again, we are speaking to everybody even if you didn't answer questions. Hi.

The Juror: Hi.
The Court: You didn't answer any questions.
The Juror: Right.
The Court: Did any questions apply to you?
The Juror: No.
The Court: Can you think of any reason that would prevent you from being fair and impartial to the Government or the defense?
The Juror: No.
The Court: Any questions?
GP: Nope.
The Court: Thank you. You can be seated.
The Juror: Thank you.
The Court: 705. 423 next. Hi. You indicated you might have a hardship?
The Juror: Yes. My son was just diagnosed with a mood disorder. He's seven. He has a doctor's appointment tomorrow and on Monday.
The Court: At what time?
The Juror: It's in the afternoon.
The Court: Like what time?
The Juror: 4:00. 4:00.
The Court: Okay. What time would you have to leave for that?
The Juror: Probably 2:30. But also my daughter has a psychotherapist—
The Court: I'm sorry?
The Juror: My daughter has one too. She has to see a psychotherapist. We're also having to consider medication with severe consequences.
The Court: Uh-huh.
The Juror: So just to—I'm afraid I might be distracted.
The Court: Hold on. I don't have any questions. Any objection?
MM: No, Your Honor.
The Court: You can go to the jury room. Thank you.
MM: 705, Your Honor?
The Court: Yes, Number 12. 423. 421 next. Hi, how are you?
The Juror: Hi.

The Court: Could you tell us about your legal experience?

The Juror: I'm currently an attorney in the Department of Justice in the criminal division. I work with the Office of International Affairs, and I've been a special at the US Attorney's Office here.

The Court: I don't have any questions.

MM: No questions, Your Honor.

The Court: Ma'am, you can go back to the jury office. Technically, the Department of Justice is prosecuting this case.

The Juror: Yeah. I mean, I don't—I don't really do, you know—

The Court: Oh, I know. But, you know, it would be like MM was in a law firm and one of his lawyers in his law firm came up.

The Juror: Do—do I get to go home?

The Court: You get to go home. Thank you. 421. 506 next. Hi. You didn't answer any questions. Did any questions apply to you?

The Juror: No.

The Court: Anything prevent you from being fair and impartial to HP or the Government?

The Juror: No.

The Court: Any questions?

The Juror: No questions.

The Court: Thank you.

The Juror: Thank you.

The Court: 506. 481 next. Hi. You indicated you might have some difficulty with the nature of the charge itself?

The Juror: My home has been burglarized, and then I was attacked. Two separate—

The Court: Okay. Tell me about your burglary.

The Juror: I live in Georgetown. My house got broken into the Tuesday after Christmas this past year.

The Court: Was anybody arrested in connection with that?

The Juror: No. No.

The Court: Okay. And tell me about the assault.

The Juror: I work for Ralph Lauren. I was attacked two years ago in the store.

The Court: Where did that occur?

The Juror: In Georgetown.

THE COURT: Was anybody arrested in connection with that?
THE JUROR: No. It was six—six guys.
THE COURT: That came in and robbed the store?
THE JUROR: Yep. Yep.
THE COURT: And you were assaulted?
THE JUROR: I was attacked, yeah.
THE COURT: And nobody was arrested?
THE JUROR: No one was arrested.
THE COURT: Can you keep those experiences separate and apart from the evidence in this case?
THE JUROR: Yes. Yes. Those were just experiences that I've had.
THE COURT: Sure. But you understand HP is presumed to be innocent?
THE JUROR: Absolutely.
THE COURT: And you have to presume him to be innocent.
THE JUROR: Yes, sir.
THE COURT: Would you be able to do that?
THE JUROR: Absolutely.
THE COURT: Okay. Good. And you indicated—can you sit on a case like this without—
THE JUROR: Sure.
THE COURT: And be fair to the Government and the defense?
THE JUROR: Absolutely.
THE COURT: Okay. Any questions?
THE JUROR: No, sir.
THE COURT: Thank you. You can be seated. 481. 171 next. Hi.
THE JUROR: Hi.
THE COURT: You didn't answer any questions. Did any questions apply to you?
THE JUROR: No.
THE COURT: Did anything prevent you from being fair and impartial?
THE JUROR: No.
THE COURT: Any questions?
Thank you. You can be seated.
Madam Court Reporter, am I going too fast? I'm saying the same thing over and over.

The Court Reporter: Not with you, just that you cut each other off.

The Court: Okay. You want me to slow it down?

The Court Reporter: And not to cut each other off.

The Court: All right. I'll make sure. Just give me the hi sign or type something in there. 171. 331 next. Right up here, ma'am. You did not answer any questions. Did any questions apply to you?

The Juror: Yes. It was my son's father who is a DC cop. He works for 6-D. He lives, like, two blocks over from Good Hope.

The Court: Okay. And he works at 6-D?

The Juror: Uh-huh.

The Court: Is this a 6-D case?

GP: It's a 7-D case.

The Court: 7-D. And is he a patrol officer or—

The Juror: Yes.

The Court: Okay. Does that make it more likely for you to believe a police officer over civilian witnesses?

The Juror: No.

The Court: Okay. Could you be fair to HP in evaluating the evidence?

The Juror: Yes.

The Court: Could you be fair to the Government?

The Juror: Yes.

The Court: Any questions?

The Juror: No.

The Court: You can be seated. 331. 086 next. Right up here. Yes, ma'am. You indicated you might live or work in the area?

The Juror: Yeah. I live over there by Anacostia Station on Wade Road.

The Court: And how far is that from the 1400-block of Good Hope Road?

The Juror: 1400-block?

The Court: How far is it away?

The Juror: It may be about twelve—

The Court: Almost a mile, right?

The Juror: Twelve—twelve blocks away.

THE COURT: Okay. Do you know the location of 1435 Good Hope Road?

THE JUROR: I believe so.

THE COURT: Have you been there, or do you know the people there?

THE JUROR: I—I grew up around there.

THE COURT: Uh-huh.

THE JUROR: So I haven't been around there in a while. But, yeah, I grew up around there.

THE COURT: Do you think your knowing the area will make it difficult for you to be fair and impartial to HP or the Government?

THE JUROR: No.

THE COURT: You can be fair to both parties?

THE JUROR: Yes.

THE COURT: Okay. Any questions?

THE JUROR: Um—

THE COURT: Thank you. You can be—oh, yes, ma'am. Did you have a question?

THE JUROR: No. Just trying to think of something. No, I can't think of anything.

THE COURT: Okay. Let us know if you do.

THE JUROR: Okay.

THE COURT: Thank you. 086. 512 next. Right up here, ma'am. You did not answer any questions. Did any questions apply to you?

THE JUROR: No.

THE COURT: Anything prevent you from being fair and impartial to HP or the Government in this case?

THE JUROR: No.

THE COURT: Any questions?

THE JUROR: No.

THE COURT: Thank you. You can be seated. 512. 584 next. Right up here, sir. Hi. How are you? You indicated either you or someone you knew had—

THE JUROR: Yes.

THE COURT: —an experience with a similar offense?

THE JUROR: Yes.

THE COURT: And what was your experience?

THE JUROR: Well, it was my daughter's experience.

THE COURT: And what was your daughter's experience?

THE JUROR: She was accosted at gunpoint and forced to march several blocks to the ATM—

THE COURT: ATM.

THE JUROR: —where he demanded that she clean out her account.

THE COURT: And where did this occur?

THE JUROR: On Capitol Hill.

THE COURT: And was anybody arrested in connection with that?

THE JUROR: I believe so, although we lost contact with the prosecutor.

THE COURT: How long ago did this occur?

THE JUROR: Just within—I mean, maybe thirteen years ago, so just marginally within your time.

THE COURT: Okay. And so, are you going to be able to keep that experience separate and apart from—

THE JUROR: Yes, absolutely, Your Honor.

THE COURT: Can you be fair to HP?

THE JUROR: Certainly.

THE COURT: Can you be fair to the Government?

THE JUROR: Certainly.

THE COURT: Any questions?

THE JUROR: No.

THE COURT: Thank you. You can be seated, sir. 584. 946 next. Right up here, ma'am. You indicated you might have a hardship?

THE JUROR: Yes. I have a doctor's appointment Monday. And this is the fourth time that I had to reschedule. The first time was—there were several reasons, very important reasons. My family and I are currently homeless. One of the reasons was to go down to housing—

THE COURT: You've got to slow down just a little. Okay, so your family is homeless, and you—your family is going to the housing authority?

THE JUROR: Yeah, we—no, we've already been to—that was one of the reasons for rescheduling my doctor's appointment.

THE COURT: What time is your doctor's appointment?

THE JUROR: Ten thirty in the morning.

The Court: Ten thirty?

The Juror: Yes.

The Court: And what time will you be through?

The Juror: Usually about an hour.

The Court: Okay. You also indicated either you or someone you knew had an experience with a similar event?

The Juror: With the assault situation. My son's father—there was a domestic violence issue.

The Court: Okay. You're going to have to slow down just a little.

The Juror: I'm sorry. It was a domestic violence issue with the father of my other two children—between him, myself, and the person that I'm currently seeing.

The Court: Okay.

The Juror: So he—he assaulted both myself and her.

The Court: Were charges brought?

The Juror: Yes.

The Court: And what happened—

The Juror: I had a CPO that recently expired this past June, but I haven't had any more contact.

The Court: So it was a civil protection order?

The Juror: Yes.

The Court: Okay.

The Juror: But it was a criminal case because the police were called.

The Court: Okay. Anything prevent you from being fair and impartial in this case against HP?

The Juror: No.

The Court: You could be fair to HP?

The Juror: Yes.

The Court: Could you be fair to the Government?

The Juror: Yes.

The Court: Okay. I will take your request under advisement. I'm not sure it's sufficient to grant you—

The Juror: I know.

The Court: But I'll talk to the lawyers.

The Juror: All right.

The Court: Thank you, ma'am.

THE JUROR: Thank you. Go sit back down?
THE COURT: Uh-huh, yes. Take—
MM: Your Honor, for the record, I move to strike on two grounds.
THE COURT: Hold on one second.
MM: Very well, Your Honor.
THE COURT: I mean, she's got a hardship. You won't let her go?
MM: It's her comment that her family is currently homeless, which kind of bothers me. It would put a lot of stress on her. And I would also object to her T-shirt, Your Honor, which said "Beat Philly," which I take personal offense to.
THE COURT: Well, you're having a tough year in that regard.
MM: Not good. 946. 717 next.
THE COURT: Right up here. Hi. You didn't answer any questions. Did any questions apply to you?
THE JUROR: I have poor English.
THE COURT: Poor English?
THE JUROR: Poor English.
THE COURT: Okay. Have you been able to understand the proceedings?
THE JUROR: No. I have back problem.
THE COURT: Okay. Hold on one second. I don't have any questions.
MM: No questions, Your Honor.
THE COURT: You can go back to the jury room.
THE JUROR: Thank you.
THE COURT: 717. 731 next. Hi. You did not answer any questions. Did any questions apply to you?
THE JUROR: No.
THE COURT: Anything prevent you from being fair and impartial in this case?
THE JUROR: I have poor English.
THE COURT: Poor English?
THE JUROR: Poor English.
THE COURT: Okay. Have you been able to understand the proceedings?
THE JUROR: No. I have back problem.
THE COURT: Okay. Hold on one second. I don't have any questions.
MM: No questions, Your Honor.
THE COURT: You can go back to the jury room.

THE JUROR: Thank you.
THE JUROR: No.
THE COURT: Any questions?
THE JUROR: Nope.
THE COURT: No.
THE COURT: Anything prevent you from being fair and impartial in this case?
THE JUROR: No.
THE COURT: Any questions?
MM: I do have a question.
THE COURT: Oh, sure.
MM: On the sheet, it listed your occupation as an attorney?
THE JUROR: That's correct.
THE COURT: What kind of law do you practice?
THE JUROR: I do health care law. I'm vice president and deputy general counsel for Bon Secours Health, which is a—
THE COURT: Thank you.
THE JUROR: —hospital system.
THE COURT: You can be seated. 065. 043 next. Hi. Right up here. You did not answer any questions. Did any questions apply to you?
THE JUROR: I don't believe so.
THE COURT: Anything prevent you from being fair and impartial in this case?
THE JUROR: I don't believe so.
THE COURT: When you say "I don't believe so," is that—
THE JUROR: I mean—
THE COURT: Is that your way of saying no?
THE JUROR: Yes. I'm sorry. Yes, that's my way of saying no.
THE COURT: Okay. Any questions? Thank you. You can be seated. 043. 868 next. Good afternoon.
THE JUROR: Good afternoon.
THE COURT: You did not answer any questions. Did any questions apply to you?
THE JUROR: The only one that applied to me that I remembered was—had somebody been robbed.

THE COURT: And have you been robbed?

THE JUROR: No. That was my cousin, yes.

THE COURT: Your cousin?

THE JUROR: Yes.

THE COURT: Where was your cousin robbed?

THE JUROR: She was in Maryland in Prince George's County.

THE COURT: And how long ago was that?

THE JUROR: That was about maybe five years ago.

THE COURT: Were you a witness to the event, or did you just hear about it?

THE JUROR: No. She just told me about it.

THE COURT: Anything prevent you from being fair to HP or the Government in this case?

THE JUROR: Um, I don't think so. I mean, I grew up near Sursum Corda around a lot of crime. So I don't know if I would be fair to say that he may have done it. I would have to hear it.

THE COURT: Right. You have to hear the evidence. But as he sits there now, you understand that he's innocent?

THE JUROR: Yeah. Yeah, of course.

THE COURT: And he remains innocent unless you're persuaded beyond a reasonable doubt that he's guilty.

THE JUROR: Right.

THE COURT: Are you going to be able to fulfill that role fairly to HP?

THE JUROR: I think so.

THE COURT: When you say "I think so," is there some hesitation in your mind?

THE JUROR: Actually, I mean, if I hear it. I'm a pretty fair person, I guess.

THE COURT: Okay. You used "I think"—is there—

THE JUROR: It's kind of contradictory, so—

THE COURT: Okay.

THE JUROR: I don't want to be making contradicting statements.

THE COURT: No, I'm not—

THE JUROR: I mean—

THE COURT: —trying to put words in your mouth.

THE JUROR: Oh, no.

THE COURT: If you have a doubt in your mind about whether you can be fair, you've got to let me know.
THE JUROR: I believe I can be fair, yeah.
THE COURT: Okay. Any questions?
THE JUROR: No.
THE COURT: Thank you. You can be seated.
THE JUROR: You're welcome.
THE COURT: 868. 778 next. Hi. You did not answer any questions. Did any questions apply to you?
THE JUROR: No.
THE COURT: Anything prevent you from being fair and impartial in this case?
THE JUROR: No. No.
THE COURT: Any questions?
THE JUROR: No.
THE COURT: Thank you. You can be seated.
THE JUROR: Uh-huh.
THE COURT: 778. 836 next. Am I doing better, Madam Court Reporter?
THE COURT REPORTER: Yes.
THE COURT: Thank you. Yes, ma'am. You indicated either you or somebody you knew had an experience with a similar offense?
THE JUROR: It wasn't a burglary. My purse got stolen about ten years ago. No weapon.
THE COURT: Where did that occur?
THE JUROR: Rhode Island Avenue Shopping Center.
THE COURT: Anything about that experience to prevent you from being fair to HP or the Government in this case?
THE JUROR: No. No.
THE COURT: Any other questions apply to you?
THE JUROR: Nope.
THE COURT: Anything to prevent you from being fair and impartial?
THE JUROR: Nope.
THE COURT: Any questions?
THE JUROR: None.
THE COURT: You can be seated.

THE JUROR: Thank you.
THE COURT: 836. 115 next.
THE JUROR: Good afternoon.
THE COURT: Hi. How are you? You did not answer any questions, sir. Did any questions apply to you?
THE JUROR: No.
THE COURT: Anything to prevent you from being fair and impartial to either side in this case?
THE JUROR: Nothing at all.
THE COURT: Any questions?
THE JUROR: None at all.
THE COURT: Thank you. You can be seated.
THE JUROR: Pleasure.
THE COURT: 115. 389 next. Hi. How are you?
THE JUROR: Fine, thanks.
THE COURT: You did not answer any questions. Did any questions apply to you?
THE JUROR: Not really.
THE COURT: Okay. Anything to prevent you from being fair to HP or the Government in this case?
THE JUROR: I don't think so, no.
THE COURT: Any questions?
THE JUROR: No.
THE COURT: Thank you. You can be seated. 389. 407 next. Hi. How are you?
THE JUROR: Fine, thanks.
THE COURT: You did not answer any questions. Did any questions apply to you?
THE JUROR: No.
THE COURT: Anything to prevent you from being fair and impartial to HP or the Government in this case?
THE JUROR: No.
THE COURT: Any questions?
THE JUROR: No.
THE COURT: Thank you. You can be seated.
MM: I have a question, Your Honor.

THE COURT: Hold on one second, ma'am. Right up here, ma'am, if you could.

MM: If you could stand up here. On the jury form, it lists your occupation as an attorney. Are you an attorney?

THE JUROR: I am.

MM: And where do you practice?

THE JUROR: The SEC here. For the government, civil lawyer.

MM: Okay. Could you say that slower?

THE JUROR: The Securities and Exchange Commission.

MM: All right. Have you ever done—

THE COURT: She said she's on the civil side.

THE JUROR: Yeah. I'm only civil. There's no criminal, so—

MM: Have you ever done any criminal work?

THE JUROR: Nope.

MM: Thank you, ma'am.

THE COURT: Thank you. 407. 114 next. Hi. Right up here. You did not answer any questions. Any questions apply to you?

THE JUROR: None.

THE COURT: Anything to prevent you from being fair and impartial to HP or the Government?

THE JUROR: No.

THE COURT: Any questions?

THE JUROR: No.

THE COURT: Thank you. You can be seated. 114. 541 next. Hi. Right up here. You indicated either you or someone you knew had an experience with a similar offense?

THE JUROR: Well, I was mugged once.

THE COURT: And when was that?

THE JUROR: 2005.

THE COURT: And where was that?

THE JUROR: Uruguay.

THE COURT: Paraguay?

THE JUROR: Uruguay.

THE COURT: Uruguay. Anything about that experience make it difficult to be fair to HP or the Government in this case?

THE JUROR: No.

THE COURT: Anything at all prevent you from being fair and impartial in this case?
THE JUROR: No.
THE COURT: Any questions?
THE JUROR: Nope.
THE COURT: Thank you. You can be seated. 541. 368 next. Hi. You did not answer any questions. Did any questions apply to you?
THE JUROR: No. I was fine with everything.
THE COURT: Anything prevent you from being fair and impartial to either side in this case?
THE JUROR: No.
THE COURT: Any questions?
THE JUROR: No.
THE COURT: Thank you. You can be seated. 368. 202 next. Hi. Right up here.
THE JUROR: Hi.
THE COURT: You indicated either you or someone you knew was associated with law enforcement?
THE JUROR: My uncle.
THE COURT: And what's your uncle's position?
THE JUROR: He's—well, he was in the Metropolitan, but now he's a sergeant for the Park Police.
THE COURT: Park Police?
THE JUROR: Um-hmmm.
THE COURT: Does that make it more likely for you to believe a police officer's testimony over someone else?
THE JUROR: No.
THE COURT: You also indicated either you or someone you knew had an experience with a similar offense?
THE JUROR: I had a cousin.
THE COURT: And what was your cousin's experience?
THE JUROR: It was robbery and assault.
THE COURT: And where did that occur?
THE JUROR: I know it was in the District.
THE COURT: Do you know when it occurred?

THE JUROR: I know it was within fifteen years. When you asked—I was younger, so I didn't know exactly—

THE COURT: But you were not a witness to the event?

THE JUROR: Uh-uh.

THE COURT: Is there anything that prevents you from being fair and impartial to HP or the Government in this case?

THE JUROR: No.

THE COURT: Any questions? Thank you, ma'am. You may be seated.

THE JUROR: Okay.

THE COURT: 202. 262 next. Hi. Right up here, ma'am. You indicated either you or someone you knew was associated with law enforcement?

THE JUROR: My niece's husband is an undercover cop.

THE COURT: And where is he a police officer?

THE JUROR: DC, I mean—I'm sorry. No, in Massachusetts.

THE COURT: Where in Massachusetts?

THE JUROR: Springfield.

THE COURT: I went to UMass, so—

THE JUROR: Oh, you did?

THE COURT: And you also indicated either—

THE JUROR: Yeah. I was in an armed bank—

THE COURT: Hold on a minute, and let me just repeat the question so the court reporter has it. You indicated either you or somebody you knew had an experience with a similar offense. Can you tell me about your experience?

THE JUROR: Okay. I was in the—there was a bank next to Metro Center, and I was in there, and they had an armed robbery.

THE COURT: And when did that occur?

THE JUROR: That was about twelve years ago.

THE COURT: Was anybody arrested in connection with that?

THE JUROR: I don't know.

THE COURT: Okay. You did not—

THE JUROR: They—

THE COURT: You did not come to court and testify?

THE JUROR: No. I don't know if they ever caught him.

THE COURT: Okay. Anything about that experience or any other factor prevent you from being fair to HP or the Government?

THE JUROR: I don't know if it would affect my—I don't know whether it would affect me or not.

THE COURT: And what causes you pause?

THE JUROR: It was a really unpleasant experience. I have to say it was bad.

THE COURT: Sure.

THE JUROR: But I don't know whether it would affect my—

THE COURT: Sure.

THE JUROR: —judgment.

THE COURT: I don't have any questions.

THE JUROR: Okay. Is that it?

THE COURT: Hold on one second.

MM: I have no questions.

THE COURT: Ma'am, you can go back to the jury room. This is probably not the best case for you to—

THE JUROR: Okay.

THE COURT: Thank you very much.

THE JUROR: Thank you.

THE COURT: 262. 467 next.

THE JUROR: Hi.

THE COURT: Hi. How are you? Could you tell us your legal experience?

THE JUROR: I was a criminal trial lawyer for ten years.

THE COURT: And where was that?

THE JUROR: Orlando, Florida.

THE COURT: And do you practice now?

THE JUROR: No.

THE COURT: Congratulations.

THE JUROR: Thank you.

THE COURT: Anything about your experience prevent you from being fair and impartial in this case?

THE JUROR: No. But, I mean, I had twenty-two jury trials. I was a public defender.

THE COURT: That's okay. Any questions?

THE JUROR: No.

THE COURT: Thank you, sir. You can be seated. 467. 054 next. Hi. Right up here.

THE JUROR: Hi.

THE COURT: You did not answer any questions. Did any questions apply to you?

THE JUROR: No, sir.

THE COURT: Anything prevent you from being fair and impartial to either side?

THE JUROR: No, sir.

THE COURT: Any questions?

THE JUROR: No, sir.

THE COURT: Thank you. You can be seated.

THE JUROR: Thanks.

THE COURT: 054. 605 next. Hi. How are you? You indicated either you or someone you knew was associated with law enforcement?

THE JUROR: Yes.

THE COURT: And who was that?

THE JUROR: I have a cousin and—well, I have one cousin that's a police officer, an uncle that's a—he does investigations for the police. And I have two cousins that work for CSOSA.

THE COURT: CSOSA?

THE JUROR: Uh-huh.

THE COURT: So you have a lot of cousins.

THE JUROR: A lot of family.

THE COURT: But you yourself are not—

THE JUROR: No.

THE COURT: —involved in law enforcement?

THE JUROR: No.

THE COURT: Does any of that relationship make it more likely for you to believe a police officer over somebody else?

THE JUROR: Um—

THE COURT: Or to favor the Government over the defense?

THE JUROR: No.

THE COURT: Okay. You also indicated that either you or someone you knew had an experience with a similar offense?

THE JUROR: Yes, my cousin. She had been robbed. They ran into her house and took everything. So I was the one she called. I mean, we're like best friends, so I went over there.

THE COURT: Okay. But you were not a witness to the event?

THE JUROR: No, I wasn't.

THE COURT: How long ago was this?

THE JUROR: Two years ago.

THE COURT: And was this in DC or somewhere else?

THE JUROR: It was right in Maryland, but she lived with me afterward. Yeah.

THE COURT: Okay. And was anybody arrested in connection with that?

THE JUROR: No.

THE COURT: So they couldn't catch anyone?

THE JUROR: No.

THE COURT: Anything about that experience make it difficult for you to be fair to HP or the Government in this case?

THE JUROR: No.

THE COURT: Okay. You could be fair to both parties?

THE JUROR: Um-hmmm.

THE COURT: Do you have any additional questions?

THE JUROR: Yes. You asked about—what did you say, fifteen years or less, as far as—well, I was convicted in Virginia for fighting, so I just wanted to make sure—

THE COURT: How long ago was that?

THE JUROR: It was like fifteen years ago, so I was twenty-five. I'm forty now.

THE COURT: That's okay.

THE JUROR: But I wanted to make sure I say it.

THE COURT: No, I appreciate that. Thanks so much.

THE JUROR: Putting it all out there.

THE COURT: Okay. You can be seated. Okay, I've got 32 so far. 605. 766 next. Hi.

THE JUROR: Hi there.

THE COURT: You indicated either you or someone you knew was associated with law enforcement?

THE JUROR: Yes. I worked for the Temple Police Department as a civilian for two years, and then I worked for the Army Criminal Investigation Division as a civilian for five.
THE COURT: And how long ago was that?
THE JUROR: I left CID two and a half years ago.
THE COURT: And—
THE JUROR: Temple was in '99 to '01.
THE COURT: Okay. You're not currently in law enforcement?
THE JUROR: Not in law enforcement. I work for a judge now.
THE COURT: Who?
THE JUROR: Judge Irwin at the Court of Appeals for the Armed Forces.
THE COURT: Oh, yeah. I used to argue cases. Does your experience make it more likely for you to favor the Government in this case over the defense?
THE JUROR: No, not at all.
THE COURT: Could you be fair to HP and the Government?
THE JUROR: Yes.
THE COURT: Any questions?
THE JUROR: No.
THE COURT: Thank you. You can be seated.
THE JUROR: Thank you.
THE COURT: 766. 655 next. Hi. You did not answer any questions. Did any questions apply to you?
THE JUROR: No.
THE COURT: Anything prevent you from being fair and impartial in this case?
THE JUROR: No.
THE COURT: Any questions?
THE JUROR: No.
THE COURT: Thank you. You can be seated.
THE JUROR: Thank you.
THE COURT: 655. 360 next. Hi. You did not answer any questions. Did any questions apply to you?
THE JUROR: No.

The Court: Anything prevent you from being fair and impartial in this case?
The Juror: No.
The Court: Any questions?
The Juror: No.
The Court: Thank you. You can be seated.
The Juror: Okay. Thank you.
The Court: 360. 182 next. Hi. How are you? You indicated you might have a hardship?
The Juror: I don't know if I would call it a hardship, but I'm in a friend's wedding this weekend in California, and I leave tomorrow. So I was a dice roller. I understand I have to come back.
The Court: So what was your—give me the schedule again. When are you leaving? Tomorrow?
The Juror: I originally left at 7:00 p.m., so I thought I had two free days, but I have a new flight. It's at 2:00 p.m.
The Court: Can you change the flight?
The Juror: No, because I'm in the wedding, so I have to be there Friday.
The Court: I don't have any questions.
MM: I don't have any questions.
The Court: You've got to go back and get a new date then. Go back to the jury room.
The Juror: I understand.
The Court: Tell them Judge Morin ordered you to get a new date.
The Juror: Okay.
The Court: Thank you.
The Juror: Thank you.
The Court: Enjoy the wedding.
The Juror: Thank you.
The Court: 182. 390 next. You did not answer any questions. Did any questions apply to you?
The Juror: No.
The Court: Anything prevent you from being fair and impartial in this case?
The Juror: No.

THE COURT: Any questions?
THE JUROR: No.
THE COURT: Thank you. You can be seated. 390. 845 next. Hi. You did not answer any questions. Did any questions apply to you?
THE JUROR: No.
THE COURT: Anything prevent you from being fair and impartial in this case?
THE JUROR: No.
THE COURT: Any questions?
THE JUROR: Nope.
THE COURT: Thank you. You can be seated.
THE JUROR: All right. Thanks.
THE COURT: 845. 799 next. Hi. How are you?
THE JUROR: Hi.
THE COURT: You indicated you might have a hardship?
THE JUROR: Yes. My parents—they live in Rhode Island, and they expect me to come home to help with a fundraiser on Sunday night, so I might not be able to get back here early enough to make the date on Monday. That would be my main concern.
THE COURT: Well, we'll probably start Monday about 11:00.
THE JUROR: That would entail me taking a plane. They live all the way out. It's a two-hour ride by train into Manhattan to take a bus down here, which is what I usually do. I can see what I can do about getting a plane, but at this point, it's kind of a big expense. I was expecting to take the bus.
THE COURT: Okay. You have jury service.
THE JUROR: But they told me about this in July.
THE COURT: Who is they?
THE JUROR: My parents told me about this in July, and I committed.
THE COURT: I know, but did you ask about your jury service?
THE JUROR: I told them about it, and they are aware of it.
THE COURT: Who is aware of it?
THE JUROR: My parents are.
THE COURT: No. I'm asking, did you ask the jury office to change your date?
THE JUROR: They told me to ask when I came in for jury duty.

THE COURT: Okay. I don't have any additional questions.
MM: No questions.
THE COURT: Ma'am, you can go back to the jury office and tell them Judge Morin ordered you to get a new date.
THE JUROR: Thank you very much.
THE COURT: You have to get a new date, and I'll check up on it.
THE JUROR: I understand that, Judge.
THE COURT: Thank you.
THE JUROR: Thank you.
THE COURT: 799. 197 next. Hi. Right up here, ma'am. You indicated you might have a hardship?
THE JUROR: Yes. I just started a new job last week, and I have conference travel this week—from Saturday to Wednesday.
THE COURT: I'm not sure that's going to make it, but I'll take it under advisement.
THE JUROR: Okay.
THE COURT: You indicated either you or someone you knew had an experience—
THE JUROR: Yeah. My brother was a victim of armed robbery, so I'm not sure how objective I can be about that, but that happened last year.
THE COURT: Were you a witness to that event?
THE JUROR: No.
THE COURT: Okay. There's no armed robbery in this case.
THE JUROR: Okay.
THE COURT: No completed robbery, but you can go back and get a new date.
THE JUROR: Okay.
THE COURT: Tell them Judge Morin ordered you to get a new date for jury service.
THE JUROR: Okay. Thank you.
THE COURT: 197. 258 next. Hi. How are you?
THE JUROR: Good. How are you?
THE COURT: You did not answer any questions. Did any questions apply to you?
(Juror nods.)

THE JUROR: I don't know. I guess I'm a little hesitant either way, but I don't know.

THE COURT: Okay. I don't have any additional questions.

MM: No questions.

THE COURT: Ma'am, anything prevent you from being fair and impartial? Anything prevent you from being fair and impartial in this case?

THE JUROR: No.

THE COURT: Any questions?

THE JUROR: No.

THE COURT: Thank you. You can be seated.

I think this is going to be the last one. 258. Hi. How are you?

THE JUROR: Fine, thank you.

THE COURT: You indicated either you or someone you knew had an experience with a similar offense?

THE JUROR: My son was involved in a robbery about ten years ago.

THE COURT: And was he the victim or charged—?

THE JUROR: He was the robber.

THE COURT: Okay. And what happened with that case?

THE JUROR: Well, he took his punishment, and now he is a very productive, wonderful citizen.

THE COURT: I'm glad to hear that.

Anything to prevent you from being fair to the Government in this case because of your son's experience?

THE JUROR: No, uh-uh.

THE COURT: Anything to prevent you from being fair to HP?

THE JUROR: No.

THE COURT: Any questions?

THE JUROR: None at all.

THE COURT: Thank you. You can be seated.

Let's go over our list now, Counsel. I think we have enough. The following jurors have been excused: On the master list, Number 3. What do you want to do with Number 6? That's the mother whose daughter was on crutches. We have enough jurors. It's up to you. I'll defer. If you both agree, we can excuse her.

MM: I have no objection to her being excused.

GP: No objection.

The Court: Okay. Number 6 will be excused.

Continue on the same page. Number 12, 13. Next page—what do you want to do with Number 21? That's the individual who had a doctor's appointment on Monday, family looking for a home. She also had a CPO against her.

MM: I move to excuse her, Your Honor.

GP: I have no objection.

The Court: Okay. Number 21 will be excused, and Number 22 is gone. Next page, I have Number 36. Next page, I have Number 43, 46, 47, and we've qualified through 48. I think this is enough. If you could just check your math. This is thirty-nine total, right?

MM: Thirty-eight, but math wasn't my strong suit.

The Court: Are we set to go?

MM: Yes, Your Honor.

The Court: Okay. I'm going to excuse the remaining jurors back to the jury office.

MM: Very well, Your Honor.

The Court: Thank you.

GP: Thank you.

(Open court.)

The Court: Ladies and gentlemen, when we call a jury panel down, we obviously do not know what the answers are going to be. I need a certain number of jurors to begin jury selection. We've reached this number, so I'm going to—will the following jurors raise their hands: 258—no, wait. Oh, wait. No. Yeah, we've got—we've qualified through 49. I apologize.

914? Ma'am?

The Juror: Yes.

The Court: And, ma'am, you and the two rows behind you can go back to the jury office at this time. Thank you for your time and service.

The Juror: Thank you.

The Court: Happy customers. Okay. Hold on one second. Juror 1—152, you may go back to the jury office. Juror 584—Juror 584, Ms. Bostic—she left.

Okay. Well—okay. Let me just check my—sir, is there an empty seat in the back row?

The Juror: Yes.

The Court: Yes, okay. Thank you.

Oh, ma'am? Juror—

The Juror: 584.

The Court: You can go back to the jury office. Thank you very much.

The Juror: Thank you.

The Court: I'm just checking my empty seats here.

Okay. Ladies and gentlemen, if you look at the jury box, the seats are numbered 1 through 6 in the front row and 7 through 14 in the back row. There are two extra seats in the back row. Now, some of you are going to be called up and asked to take a seat. Just take the seat you've been asked to sit in. Some of you may not come up at all. Some of you will come up and go down. Some of you will come up, go down, go back, some two or three times.

Try not to follow it from your point of view. It doesn't make much sense. Just listen for your number and the seat number. At a certain point, it's over, and I'll let you know who is on the jury.

The Deputy Clerk: Could Juror Number 506 please step forward and take seat number 3 in the jury box. That's the one in the front row closest to the judge.

Could Juror 481 please step forward and take seat number 6. That's the seat right there on the end in the front row.

Could Juror 171 come and sit in seat number 12 in the jury box. That's the one closer to the judge in the back row.

And could Juror 331 please step forward and take the remaining seat in the jury box. Thank you.

The Court: Counsel can approach the clerk.

The alternates are 7 and 8. And just put that in the seat so they know.

Ladies and gentlemen, if you're in the box and the clerk asks you to take a seat in the audience, if you can take a seat in the last row all the way to the wall, jurors will be filling in those last two rows.

THE DEPUTY CLERK: Could Juror 619 from the jury box please take a seat in the gallery.

THE COURT: Back all the way to the wall, sir. Thank you very much.

THE DEPUTY CLERK: Could Juror 506 also have a seat in the gallery, and Juror 171, if you could also take a seat in the gallery.

Could Juror 086 please step forward and take seat number 3 in the jury box.

Could Juror 717 please step forward and take seat number 4 in the jury box.

And could Juror 731 please step forward and take seat number 12 in the jury box.

THE COURT: That was 731? Okay.

THE DEPUTY CLERK: Yes, 731.

THE COURT: Thank you.

THE DEPUTY CLERK: Um-hmmm.

Could Juror 731 please take a seat in the gallery.

And could Juror 065 please step forward and take seat number 12 in the jury box.

Could Juror 420 please take a seat in the audience? And could Juror 868 please step forward and take a seat in the jury box?

THE COURT: Ladies and gentlemen in the box, you'll be our jury in this matter. Now that you find yourselves on the jury, does anyone wish to bring anything to my attention that may prevent you from sitting through the conclusion of the case?

(Juror raises hand.)

THE COURT: Yes, sir, come up here.

(Bench conference.)

THE COURT: You have to wait for the lawyers. Come on up. First of all, could I have your number, please?

THE JUROR: 105.

THE COURT: And this is the juror in seat number 9. Yes, sir.

THE JUROR: Oh, I answered all the questions truthfully, but I thought you and the attorneys should know that what I do for a living, I cover Prince George's County Courts for the *Washington Post*.

THE COURT: Right. You're a reporter?

THE JUROR: Yeah. I have written a lot about those issues and all of that.

THE COURT: I appreciate that. Thank you very much. You can be seated.

MM: Can I ask a follow-up question?

THE COURT: Sure.

MM: Obviously, we would like to know if that would affect your ability to judge this case fairly?

THE JUROR: I—I don't think so. I mean, I think I judge facts.

MM: Okay.

THE COURT: Thanks so much.

I mean, to me, he is qualified. If you mutually agree you want him off, that's fine.

GP: I would ask that he be dismissed.

MM: I don't object. I don't object to—I'm just concerned. A writer is a writer, and it's hard not to be a writer.

THE COURT: That's fine. There's a difference between consenting and not objecting. Do you also want him off?

MM: Yes.

THE COURT: Okay. So both parties want him off?

MM: Yes.

GP: Yes.

THE COURT: Okay.

(Open court.)

THE COURT: Sir, you're excused from the jury at this time. Thank you very much.

Call the next juror, please.

THE DEPUTY CLERK: Could Juror 836 please step forward and take seat number 9 in the jury box?

THE COURT: Welcome aboard. I'll repeat my question. Now that you find yourself on the jury, does anyone wish to bring anything to my attention that may prevent you from sitting through the conclusion of the case?

Thank you. This is the third time I've asked the question, so—ladies and gentlemen in the audience, that completes jury selection in this matter. My congratulations or condolences, depending on whether you wanted to get on. You can be excused back to the jury office at this time. Thank you for your time and effort.

Let me just speak to the lawyers for a second.

(Bench conference.)

THE COURT: I'll defer to you. I mean, we have forty-five minutes. We can get started. I mean, it's forty-five minutes we don't have to worry about on another day. It's up to you. I know it's been a long day. I know jury selection is taxing.

MM: My feeling is, since it's so close to the end of the day, my preference, I should say, Your Honor, would be to begin with openings tomorrow right before the evidence. I know mine will be short either way.

GP: I agree with that, Your Honor.

THE COURT: Okay. The way I operate, if you both consent to these procedural matters, you just nod to each other and let me know—

GP: Okay.

THE COURT: —you're both requesting it. I'm not here to grind people down, I'm here to get the trial done.

MM: Thank you, Your Honor. I appreciate that.

THE COURT: So I know jury selection—you have a lot of information coming at you, and I tend to go a little more efficiently than others, so—more rapid.

GP: Interesting.

MM: Interesting way to describe it, Your Honor. I would not say unfair, but efficient. I would agree.

THE COURT: I think my—

MM: No, it's not unfair.

THE COURT: I get—

MM: Very efficient.

THE COURT: Close people, do I not?

MM: Uber efficient.

THE COURT: Okay. So I'll excuse the jury.

I have fourteen matters tomorrow. I probably won't get started until 10:45 or 11:00. Do you have calendar matters tomorrow? Will you be able to make it?

GP: Yeah, 10:45 is not a problem.

THE COURT: Okay. Now, you're going to have to have your witnesses circling like airplanes around Kennedy Airport on a foggy day.

GP: If it's anything like I just experienced, they'll be here.

THE COURT: Okay. Thank you.

GP: Thank you.

MM: Thank you.

(Open court.)

THE COURT: Okay, ladies and gentlemen, I was just talking to the lawyers. Let me tell you a bit—a little bit about how Superior Court operates so that you understand the sort of schedule. We're required by the chief judge's order to recess at 4:45. That's when our overtime kicks in, so we cannot go past 4:45 on the dot. So it takes the clerk about fifteen minutes to get you set up and explain what's going to happen, so we're talking about maybe half an hour or twenty minutes of opening statements, which may cut the opening statements in half. So rather than do that, I'm going to start tomorrow morning.

So a couple of general instructions: First of all, always wear your juror badge so people know that you're a juror. Lawyers, participants in the trials are on guard—they've been told to watch for people with a juror's badge. So you have to have your juror badge. You're no longer going to enter the courtroom the way you did this afternoon. You're going to enter through the secured corridors directly back to the jury room each time you report. So you no longer come into the courtroom; you just go right to the jury room when you assemble. When all fourteen of you are there, just knock on the door. We won't answer the door—that just indicates that all fourteen of you are there, and we know that you've assembled.

During the course of the trial, you can't go on any—you can't go on the Internet to try to do your investigation. You can't go on social media to discuss the case. You can't go—I'm always getting this thing—Facepage?

THE JURY: Facebook.

THE COURT: I'm sorry—Facebook? Facebook. You can't go on Facebook and make posts. The whole idea is you cannot communicate with anyone during the course of the trial because you're going to decide it based solely on the evidence and without discussing it with anybody else, or even discussing it among yourselves. We do not want you to begin discussing the case until all the evidence is in and you've heard the final instructions. Now, that also means—we had a trial once where I gave the jury the same instruction and discovered during deliberations that some juror was investigating something on the Internet through their child, thinking that, "Since I'm not doing it personally, I'll just have my child go on the Internet and research things." Obviously, you can't do that either.

If any of you need—so each day, let's talk about the days. We have about twenty cases each day we have to get through before we start the jury trial, so we're going to bring you in somewhere between 10:30 and 11:00 each day. We take a luncheon recess about 1:00, wherever the trial may break naturally, and we recess each day at 4:45. The only time that schedule changes is when you're deliberating. If you are deliberating, you're not waiting for the Court, so you come in at 9:30, take a luncheon recess at 1:00, and you recess at 4:45.

Those of you who need written confirmation of your jury service for your employer or teacher, just let the clerk know, and he'll provide you with written confirmation. Other than that, we're going to provide you with some information—contact information—something in case something comes up. It's very important for you to be on time because if you're not on time, we have to wait for you, and you're holding up everyone in the trial. So just be mindful of that.

We're very mindful of the fact that we're taking you out of your daily lives, so when you're back there, we're in here trying to make the trial more streamlined and discussing issues to see how we can shorten it. The lawyers know that having jurors wait around is not the way to go.

So during the course of jury service, again, you can't talk to anybody, you can't write to anybody, you can't do your own investigation, you can't go to this area and do your own investigation. So we're going to begin the trial tomorrow—when did I say? 10:45?

The Deputy Clerk: 10:45.

The Court: Do you think we can get it done by then?

The Deputy Clerk: Yeah.

The Court: 10:45. 10:45. So be here. Mr. Phillips is going to go with you now. He's going to be in charge of you, and he's going to take you back to the jury room and answer some of the more practical questions you may have about whether you can bring food or drink and stuff like that. And he'll go over any questions you may have. We look forward to your service. We'll see you tomorrow morning at 10:45. Thank you.

The Jury: Thank you, Your Honor.

(Jury out.)

The Court: Okay. As a general operating rule, if you have preliminary matters, you have to email each other beforehand, and you have to email the Court so that I know what issues may be arising. So if you have any issues, preliminary matters, email them to the Court—any cases you want me to look at. But also, the general rule is, you can't raise a matter for the first time without discussing it with the other party first. See if you can resolve it, so—

MM: Very well, Your Honor.

GP: Yes, sir.

The Court: Try to resolve—

MM: Can we have the chambers' email address, Your Honor?

The Court: Yeah. Get that from Mr. Phillips.

MM: Very well, Your Honor.

THE COURT: Other than that, you can go anywhere in the courtroom. You don't have to ask permission to go anywhere. I'd like you to review the exhibits with one another. If you're not going to have any objection to the exhibits, just state that to the other side. You can display them at any time during the examination if you know there's not going to be an objection to the exhibits, including opening statements. The only restriction is, if I think you're being too close or too unfair to a witness, I'll ask you to back up. Other than that, I do not supervise your actions in the courtroom. I assume you'll do what you're going to do.

GP: Thank you, Your Honor.

THE COURT: Anything else?

MM: I guess there's one final issue. I was going to ask the Court if the Court would encourage the Government to provide the defense with Jencks tonight, since it's going to be such a speedy trial—

GP: I have Jencks—I have Jencks already prepared for Counsel.

THE COURT: Thank you very much. I appreciate that.

MM: I have no doubt, Your Honor.

THE COURT: If you anticipate any nonstandard or unusual Red Book instructions, or non–Red Book instructions, if you can email them to me, I can start loading them up. I would ask, if you're going to have a defense theory of the case, email it to the Court. I won't disclose it to the Government until you give me authority to do so. But I would like to start—there's going to be a lot of instructions. Let me hear your proposal on felon in possession.

MM: My proposal would be a bifurcated trial, Your Honor. I guess what we used to call a stipulated trial. In other words, the jury doesn't hear evidence of the prior felony, but it hears evidence, obviously, of the possession.

THE COURT: So the way it's been handled by me in the past, upon request, is I have you fill out a written jury waiver form on the element of felon in possession.

MM: Felon, right.

THE COURT: And is there a UF and a UA in this case?

GP: There—there is, Your Honor.

THE COURT: Okay. You're going forward on all the charges?

GP: Yes.

The Court: Okay. So handle it like that. Is that what you're proposing?

MM: It is, Your Honor.

The Court: So you would submit that issue to the Court, the felon in possession to the Court?

MM: Correct, Your Honor.

The Court: Okay. So I would be inclined to sever it out, have him sign a jury waiver form. And then you understand it's an independent decision by the Court—

MM: Yes, Your Honor.

The Court: —if it's severed. Regardless of what the jury does, I can render an independent decision on the felon in possession.

MM: Correct, Your Honor. Is there a name for that procedure, Your Honor?

The Court: Well, technically, it would be a severance and a bench trial.

MM: I see.

The Court: If you want a jury trial on it, I'm going to submit it to the jury. I'm not trying to talk you into one way or the other. That's—

MM: I was just wondering the name. The procedure that Your Honor described would be the one I would request.

The Court: Well, think about it. You can discuss it with HP. I mean, I've had it—I must tell you, I've been convinced over the course that juries decide it, whether they find out about the felon in possession or they don't. If you want the felon in possession submitted to the jury, my general procedure in that regard is the Government is not allowed to mention it in opening statements. Presumably, this is a stipulation. It's the last piece of evidence the Government introduces.

A cautionary instruction is given at that time, and the Government is instructed not to focus on that element in its closing argument with another cautionary instruction at the end. So those are sort of the alternatives that people have requested. I would say more recently defense counsel or the same thing with the latter, but I—you know, you can discuss that with HP.

MM: I will.

The Court: Those are your options.

GP: Thank you, Your Honor.

The Court: Thank you. We do move, okay?

GP: I can see that, Your Honor.

The Court: It's only because I think it's more effective in front of a jury when they know their time is being used efficiently.

GP: Yes, Your Honor.

The Court: So you can discuss that process with GP and come to—

MM: I will.

The Court: —whatever conclusion you come to.

(Proceedings adjourned at approximately 4:13 p.m.)

CERTIFICATE OF REPORTER

I, Kristin Gilliam, an Official Court Reporter for the Superior Court of the District of Columbia, do hereby certify that I reported, by machine shorthand, in my official capacity, the proceedings had and testimony adduced upon the jury trial in the case of the *UNITED STATES OF AMERICA versus HP*, Criminal Action Number 2011-CF3-8205, in said court on the twelfth day of October 2011.

I further certify that the foregoing 91 pages constitute the official transcript of said proceedings, as taken from my machine shorthand notes, together with the backup tape of said proceedings, to the best of my ability.

In witness whereof, I have hereto subscribed my name, this the twenty-eighth day of March 2012.

Kristin Gilliam
Official Court Reporter

Superior Court of the District Of Columbia
Criminal Division
United States of America v. HP, Defendant
Criminal Action No. 2011-CF3-8205
Volume 2 of 2
Washington, DC
Thursday, October 13, 2011

The above-entitled action came on for a jury trial before the Honorable Robert E. Morin, Associate Judge, in courtroom number 312.

This transcript represents the product of an official reporter, engaged by the court, who has personally certified that it represents the testimony and proceedings of the case as recorded.

Appearances:

On behalf of the Government: GP, Esquire, Assistant United States Attorney

On behalf of the Defendant: MM, Esquire, Washington, DC

Kristin Gilliam
Official Court Reporter

TABLE OF CONTENTS

WITNESSES

For the Government:

For the Defendant:

Exhibits

For the Government:

Exhibit	Admitted
Exhibit 15, 16	123
Exhibit 6	133
Exhibit 10	137
Exhibit 13	226

For the Defendant:

Exhibit	Admitted
(No entries provided)	—

Miscellany

THE DEPUTY CLERK: Calling from Your Honor's trial calendar, *United States v. HP*, Case Number 2011-CF3-8205.

GP: Good morning, Your Honor. GP for the United States.

MM: Good morning, Your Honor. MM for HP.

THE COURT: MM?

MM: Yes, Your Honor.

THE COURT: Your decision?

MM: With regard to the—

THE COURT: Felon in possession.

MM: Yes, Your Honor. I'd like to go with the—I discussed it with my client—the severance option.

THE COURT: Okay. Could you give him a jury waiver form, please.

HP, you understand you do have a right to a jury trial on the issue of the charge of felon in possession. I indicated—your lawyer has indicated, and you've signed a form indicating you are waiving your right to a jury trial in that matter. We have picked a jury.

You've seen the jury that we've picked. You do have the right to present this charge to the jury and have the jury make the decision, but by your signature and your waiver, you're asking the Court to make that decision. Is that correct? You have to answer out loud.

THE DEFENDANT: Yes, sir.

THE COURT: Okay. Did anybody force you or coerce you into entering the decision?

THE DEFENDANT: Naw.

THE COURT: Now, you understand that the Court will decide the case independent of the jury's verdict. So if, for example, the jury hangs—it's a mistrial—or the jury finds you not guilty of all the charges, it would still be up to the Court to make an independent judgment about the charge of felon in possession, and it is not decided by the jury. Do you understand that?

THE DEFENDANT: Yes, Your Honor.

THE COURT: And do you still want to waive your right to a jury trial on that matter?

THE DEFENDANT: Yes, Your Honor.

THE COURT: Did anybody force you or coerce you into making that decision?

THE DEFENDANT: No, Your Honor.

THE COURT: I find the defendant freely and voluntarily waived his right to a jury trial on the charge of felon in possession, and that will be tried separately to the Court. Both can incorporate the evidence presented at the jury trial, and then once the jury trial is over, we'll conclude the proceedings on that charge.

GP: Yes, sir.

THE COURT: Thank you. Any other preliminary matters?

MM: There are, Your Honor, a number—I think we've worked a lot of them out.

THE COURT: Good. But you're supposed to email me if there were any preliminary matters.

MM: Sorry, Your Honor, but I—I discovered them well into the early hours of the morning.

There's a photograph which we have to take a look at. There's a photograph on a camera of a woman, who is unknown to me and unknown to my client, holding some guns. The defendant would object to that. We've gone over all the other evidence.

THE COURT: Okay. Well, all I'll ask you is not to display that until you lay a foundation for it.

GP: Yes, Your Honor.

THE COURT: And we can determine the relevance.

MM: There are two more issues, Your Honor.

THE COURT: Yes.

MM: One is a 911 call, which was made by the complainant in this case, JH, where he gives a false name but then says something to the effect that HP just shot at JH. I don't believe it falls into the category of an excited utterance. It may be a statement of identification, but it is rather lengthy. There are two calls, and there are a lot of things in the 911 call that are not statements of—

THE COURT: Hold on. You just found out about the 911 call this morning?

MM: No, Your Honor, I did not.

THE COURT: Right. So that could have been an issue we addressed some time ago, could we not?

MM: It could have, Your Honor.

THE COURT: Thank you.

MM: And the third—I did just find out, actually, a few hours ago—is a videotaped statement of MB, a nine-year-old child, who was interviewed for a period of about, I guess, a little bit over an hour. And I would intend to use that video to impeach him on cross. However, it is produced on a special program. In other words, it can only be played on the program that comes with the disc, and that disc has a—I guess—a manufacturing defect in that you can't fast-forward, and you can't pinpoint times. So, in order for me to efficiently impeach him with what is in the video, we have to wait an inordinate amount of time in open court. But we've talked about it, and we have a proposed solution, Your Honor.

THE COURT: Um-hmmm.

MM: Which would be that I—I impeach him on what they ask him, the questions—

THE COURT: That's assuming it's—

MM: Assuming, of course.

THE COURT: —assuming he's impeached.

MM: Of course. Of course.

THE COURT: All right.

MM: Yes, Your Honor.

There are six or seven issues I do expect, however, will come up. And I have flagged them, and I have the times flagged. And what I intend to do, by agreement with the Government, is then ask him the question, "On this day, didn't you say this at this interview?" If he says, "Yes," I'm done. If he says, "No," then in my view, it's for impeachment. And then GP and I will get together and consent and see if we agree whether it's fertile for impeachment. Then I will be able to use some video-editing software to pull out.

THE COURT: Sounds like a very reasonable solution. I appreciate it.

GP: Or we may even be able to stipulate—

THE COURT: Correct.

GP: —as to what the inconsistencies are.

THE COURT: Either way. You can make a decision.

MM: I should have—I probably wouldn't agree to stipulate as to what the inconsistencies were. I'd rather have the jury see it.

THE COURT: Totally understandable. But I'll—you have two solutions, and either one is fine with the Court.

MM: Very well, Your Honor.

THE COURT: 911 call—are you planning on introducing the entire call?

GP: I do, Your Honor. And it's the Government's position that this is a 911 call just like any other 911 call. The witness is clearly available for cross-examination, and secondly, it goes to ID. So, for a couple of reasons, there is no basis to exclude this call.

MM: I completely agree when it comes to the ID, Your Honor.

THE COURT: Okay.

MM: But there's a lot more in that call. There are two of them, for one, and it describes the event. To the extent it's ID, I don't object.

THE COURT: Okay. So it would be introduced on an identification basis. Are you saying there are portions you want redacted?

MM: I'm saying that the Government intends on introducing, if my understanding is correct, the entire 911 call, and I would—I would object to that as hearsay, regardless of whether he's—

THE COURT: This is why I would like to be alerted, because I could have listened to the 911 call and made some decisions without holding up the trial.

MM: I won't add insult to injury by offering an excuse, Your Honor.

THE COURT: No, no, no. I'm—I'm not—I'm just making an observation so that in the future you understand why I try to do it that way.

MM: I do, Your Honor.

THE COURT: How long are the 911 calls?

GP: One is very short, under a minute, and then the second one is probably two and a half minutes to three. And I will say to the Court that there are some portions of the call that—that don't really benefit the Government. The first is: JH failed to identify who he is. In fact, he gives a false name.

THE COURT: Right. I'm assuming—

GP: So there are portions that I really wouldn't like to—to see come in to begin with. But having said that, we intend to play the whole tape.

THE COURT: Right. I just have to listen to it, that's all I'm saying. So is that—is that something I can listen to over lunchtime, or were you planning on introducing it this morning?

GP: What time does the Court plan to break?

THE COURT: 1:00.

GP: 1:00. It can wait until then.

THE COURT: Okay. And I'll listen to it over lunch, and we'll hear further arguments. Anything else?

MM: No, Your Honor.

THE COURT: Thank you.

GP: Your Honor, may I have a moment to set up the—

THE COURT: No, no. You do whatever you want. Thank you.

(Brief recess.)

THE DEPUTY CLERK: Calling from Your Honor's trial calendar, *United States v. HP*, Case Number 2011-CF3-8205.

MM: MM for HP, Your Honor.

GP: Good morning again, Your Honor. GP for the United States.

THE COURT: You're—you're going to give an opening?

MM: I am, Your Honor.

THE COURT: Okay.

(Jury in.)

THE COURT: Good morning, ladies and gentlemen.

THE JURY: Good morning.

THE COURT: All set.

(Jury panel sworn.)

THE COURT: Ladies and gentlemen, your taking the oath actually officially starts the jury trial. We have pads and pens for you. Feel free to take notes. Be mindful of the fact that we do not have the ability to produce a transcript for you of testimony, so you have to rely on your memory. So feel free to take notes. You'll just leave them on your seat during the trial. Nobody looks at them, and you'll be able to take your notes back with you during your deliberation. Again, I'm going to remind you: We do not have the ability to produce a transcript for you, so you have to rely on your memory.

If, during the course of the trial, I sustain an objection, that means you disregard the question; do not speculate as to what the answer would have been. I remind you that HP, as he sits there, is presumed to be innocent, and it's the Government's burden to prove him guilty beyond a reasonable doubt.

At this time, we're going to hear opening statements. Let me instruct you that opening statements are not evidence in the case. They are statements by the lawyers as to what they believe the evidence will show.

GP: Thank you, Your Honor, Counsel. Good morning.

THE JURY: Good morning.

THE COURT: Ladies and gentlemen, reasonable people tend to settle disputes with extended family members by reasonable means. But, unfortunately, in this scenario, it just didn't work out that way. The evidence will show, ladies and gentlemen, that this man, HP, because of a minor skirmish between two dogs, armed himself with a handgun and invaded, with another man, the home of a woman who was unrelated to HP, rushed inside that home, and shot that gun numerous times while there were kids inside that house. And he did so, ladies and gentlemen, with the specific intent to intimidate and frighten his first cousin, JH.

Now, you'll hear from JH a bit later on today. And JH will tell you—by the way, JH—JH, by his own admission and by judgment of most people in our community, would not be considered a pillar of our society. You see, JH is a convicted felon. In fact, JH will not be walking into this courtroom through that door like many of us do; JH will be coming from that door, because he is currently facing a criminal charge of his own. But having said that, and despite JH's personal transgressions, JH will come in, and he will tell you about an incident that was wholly uncalled-for and unwarranted. JH will tell you that on April 27 of this year, he was essentially homeless. And he had a friend that he referred to as Ree-Ree, whose real name is MB. MB lives at 1435—or lived at the time—at 1435 Good Hope Road, Southeast. And Ree Ree, who has a big heart, offered her place for JH to lay his head, and she would do that from time to time. Well, on this particular day, JH will tell you that he spent the night at the home of MB in the basement. JH will tell you that next door to MB's home, just by chance, is a barbershop which is owned by his brother, MS And he will tell you that his brother has two dogs, two big dogs, each one weighing at least 150 pounds, and that his brother, MS, keeps these dogs in the backyard in a couple of kennels, mainly for security purposes. JH will tell you that he loves these dogs, that he cares for these dogs when his brother isn't around, and that these dogs care a lot about JH. He will tell you that during the early morning hours of April 27, while he was asleep in the house at 1435, next door to where the dogs were kept, the dogs made a lot of noise. In fact, so much noise that it disturbed the folks living at 1435. And as a result, JH got up. We're talking about 3:00, maybe 4:00 in the morning. He got up, went outside, went next door, and gathered the dogs up. Now two dogs: one is named Adam, and one is named—guess what?

THE JURY: Eve.

GP: Very good.

He takes Adam and Eve for a walk because he figures if he takes them out, gives them a little exercise, maybe they'll settle down and go to sleep. So he did that. He takes the dogs. He walks through the neighborhood. But he makes one small mistake, and that is he holds one of the dogs by the leash, and he permits the other dog to walk free. He ends up, ladies and gentlemen, in the 1300 block of Valley Place Southeast, which is just a few blocks away. But this block happens to be where HP lives, who, again, is JH's first cousin. It also was the former residence of HP's beloved grandmother. And HP's grandmother owned a dog as well, except this dog was a poodle, and this dog's name is Grady. And just like Adam and Eve, everybody loved Grady. Grady was a sweet dog—is a sweet dog. So JH finds himself walking in the 1300 block of Valley Place, and it's a quiet night. Movement can be easily detected on the street.

And it just so happens that Grady, instead of being in the house, where she normally would be—or he normally would be—is outside on the front porch. And when Grady hears the two dogs and JH approach, Grady starts barking. And when Grady begins to bark, that, in turn, alerts Adam and Eve. One of the dogs is walking free, takes the opportunity to bound down the street and up on the porch, and then, unfortunately, bites—but not severely—Grady.

JH rushes over to the house, gathers up his dogs, checks on Grady. And by this time, there's an occupant inside 1362 looking out, another cousin of JH's, a cousin of HP, a guy by the name of NW. NW sees what's going on outside, and he threatens JH. JH gathers his dogs, and he walks away. He goes back to the 1400 block of Good Hope Road. He puts the dogs in the kennel, and he goes to sleep.

Fast-forward between 9:00 a.m. and 10:00 a.m., same day. JH looks out the window and sees HP approach the house with JH's uncle. MB is up and walking around the house. She answers the door. The uncle wants to know where JH is. JH comes down when he sees HP and the other gentleman approach the house, and he begs MB not to let them in.

Quote/unquote, "If you do, there's going to be some bullshit."

MB says, "JH is not here." But she notices HP has gone around the side of the house toward the basement door. And what she also notices is that Mr.—HP has a gun at his side, a black gun. And he wants to know, "Where is JH? Because when I find JH, I'm going to kill him, and then I'm going to spit on his grave."

They leave. MB is upset. She confronts JH. "What the hell is going on? What did you do, JH?" JH explains about the dog incident.

Fast-forward again, about 1:30 same day. JH again notices through the window that HP is back. This time he's with NW. There are a couple of young girls in the house; they answer the door. All they could hear from outside were demands for JH. And ultimately, the statement, "If you don't open this door, I'm going to kick it in."

MB comes downstairs, hearing the ruckus, looks out the side window along—adjacent to the door.

She sees HP, and she sees the other gentleman. And the next thing she knows, bam, the door is kicked in; it flies open. HP with a gun, NW with a gun, rush inside the house.

MB is hysterical at this point, grabs up her one son—twelve-year-old son—rushes out the front door of the house into the street.

(Audio interruption.)

MM: My apologies, Your Honor.

GP: I think he did that intentionally.

The Court: No.

MM: I apologize, GP.

GP: No problem.

She rushes outside. She makes a 911 call. She's frantic because she has left her other children in the house. Primarily, she's left her nine-year-old son, MB, in her bedroom, and she just heard gunshots inside her own house. So you can imagine her state of mind. These two men rush up the stairs, onto the second floor, and into a room that leads to the attic. When they reach the second floor, around the attic area, HP, with his gun pointed in the direction of his first cousin, JH, discharges four rounds. Fortunately, he does not strike anyone. But, again, you can only imagine the fright, fear, and trepidation that this action has caused to JH, not to mention the little boy in the house.

Speaking of MB, when these four shots were fired, the two men ran back downstairs. But before they reached the steps to the landing to go downstairs, MB is in his mom's bedroom. And he looks in that direction where he heard the gunshots, and he sees a person that he knows from the neighborhood, and he knows him as HP—HP. And he sees HP standing in his house, holding a gun and wearing purple shorts.

HP and NW leave the house. They jump into a black SUV with what some people refer to as spinners. Spinners are rims that keep spinning even when the car is at a standstill, very distinctive in appearance. MB remembered those things. They flee the neighborhood. Later that day, approximately 6:00 p.m., the police interview MB. During the course of the interview, they present to MB what's called a photo array or a photo spread. And they give MB an opportunity to point out the individual that was responsible for invading her home. And without hesitation, she points to photograph number 8, which is the photograph of HP. Shortly thereafter, police officers show the same photo array to MB. MB, as did his mother, pointed to photograph number 8 as the person that he saw holding the firearm in his house. Number 8 is a photograph of HP.

JH, who goes by the name JH in the community, was given an opportunity as well several days later to look at what we refer to as a confirmation photograph, just one photograph because this is his first cousin. He knows who he is. He was shown that confirmation photograph of HP, and he immediately identified HP as the person that burst inside of the home and shot the gun in his direction. As to 1362 Valley Place, ladies and gentlemen, a search warrant was executed in that home. The room in which HP occupied was searched, and inside that room—this was two days after the incident—inside that room was recovered a pair of purple shorts, along with a variety of other purple-in-color garments.

Ladies and gentlemen, all the Government asks you to do in this case is to be fair to both sides, apply your common sense and the law that will be—that you'll be instructed on by Judge Morin a bit later in the trial. And if you're able to do that, the Government is confident that there is but one conclusion you can reach in this matter, and that is guilty of each and every charge of the indictment.

Thank you, ladies and gentlemen.

MM: GP, Your Honor, ladies and gentlemen of the jury, once again, my name is MM, and I represent HP. Although his name is spelled a little unusually, it's pronounced HP.

I would respectfully disagree with GP on what this trial is going to show and the kind of evidence that you're going to see. I would even disagree that it's going to be a case or a story, if you will, about some sort of family feud. What it's about is—His Honor is going to instruct you at the very end of this case—is about whether the Government has proven beyond a reasonable doubt whether HP entered that property on Good Hope Road and discharged a weapon, as some of the Government witnesses will say. Reasonable doubt—you're going to learn throughout the course of this case, particularly at the end of this case—is the highest proof of standard in our criminal justice system, the very highest. And the Government's case, the evidence that they're going to put on, is going to fall far short of it. You are going to hear from JH, who goes by the name JH, the Government's star witness. But I disagree with GP on the—the sort of nature of the testimony that he's going to give. What you're going to learn is that when the police first arrive at the house on Good Hope Road, what JH told the police is that he heard some shots and that he jumped out a window, and that he didn't see anyone.

You're going to learn that he was hiding in the backyard. You're going to learn that he was hiding in the backyard, not from anyone in the house. He was hiding in the backyard because he felt the police were going to come, and he was afraid that he had a warrant. You're going to learn that he made statements to the police that he jumped out, didn't see who the shooter was, and ran from the house, and you're going to receive evidence in the case from JH himself that he wasn't attempting to protect his cousin, HP, because indeed, at that point, he told the police that he thought it was HP and that HP had a beef with him and was out to get him for some prior event.

You're going to learn that he's testified throughout the course of this case consistent with what GP said, that he was chased up into the attic, and that while in the attic, HP fired a number of shots at him. But you're also going to learn that he gave a statement after that completely changing his story to a defense investigator, saying this time that he was down in the basement. He heard the shots, he came upstairs, and he walked outside.

By the time we get to trial, which we're in, in a few minutes, I have to—I have to admit, I don't know what JH is going to say because you're going to learn he changed his story so many times. We're really and truly just going to have to wait and see.

The Government's other witness—of three supposed eyewitnesses—is MB. MB, you're going to learn, owned that house and allowed Jo-Jo to live in a bedroom in that house. And—and she is going to get on the stand and testify that she walked up to the front door, that she looked out a little window that is just to the right of the front door. And she's going to testify on the stand, under oath right in front of you folks, probably within a few hours, that she saw HP. But what you're also going to hear is that she had a number of contacts with police and made statements to police prior to her testimony, obviously, on the stand today. You're going to learn that her first statement to police was by way of a 911 call. In the middle of this, you're going to hear her voice. You're going to hear how excited she is. You're going to hear that she is under the influence of a traumatic event of knowing that someone was in her house discharging weapons, and you're going to hear them ask her, "Who is it?" And you're going to hear her in this excited state say, "I don't know. I don't know."

You're going to hear them ask for a description, and she's not going to be able to give any, because she says she doesn't know. She repeats she doesn't know who it was.

You're going to learn that the police arrived some minutes later and interviewed her just moments after. Same thing. They asked her who it was, and she tells them she doesn't know. You're going to learn that it was only after she was some ten to fifteen feet from another police officer—two police officers, actually—were discussing that they heard the name HP from a nine-year-old boy who was in the house, that she changed her story and said, "Yes, it was HP." And that's the story she stuck with ever since.

MB, you're going to learn—nine-year-old MB—you're going to see him. He's a sweet kid, and he loves his mom. And he's going to get up on the stand, and he's going to try to tell you in his, I guess, nine-year-old way of what happened. And what you're going to hear MB say is that he was up in bed, actually asleep about noon because he's a kid, and he's asleep. He says he hears gunshots. And what does he do? In one version of the stories that he's given, he goes right under the covers.

You're going to hear JH testify that after he came down from the attic again, one of his stories, he goes right into the room to find that's exactly where MB is, you're going to hear. "Under the covers." He hears shots, and he goes under the covers.

But MB also states that he looked out the room into the hallway, and that he saw two individuals. And like everyone else in the house, MB is going to say that both of them had guns. He's going to say that they're running down the hall, and he is going to say that one of those persons was HP. None of these people saw who the shooter was in the house.

With regard to JH, at the end of this case, you're not going to know what his story is because you're going to hear so many.

With regard to MB, same story. The stories change. They didn't see who the shooter was in the house. But there is something that all three of the Government's civilian witnesses do have in common: All three of them knew HP prior to this event. All three of them knew that there was an ongoing beef—an argument, if you will—between HP and JH. All of them knew it. All of them knew, prior to this, that HP did, from time to time, travel around in a black truck or a black SUV. And all of them—all of them—knew that he was fond, if you will, of the color purple, that he wore purple all of the time. All of them had the information that they would need to give these statements to the police prior to this event, and the motivation. If you take a look at

MB: someone shooting in her house, JH suspecting that it's HP because he knows he has this beef, but telling the police that he didn't see the shooter. All of them had the motivation and the opportunity to tell the police that it was HP. But, you know, at the end of this trial, I'm not going to stand up and argue to you what I think happened. I'm not going to ask you to make your decision based on what you believe happened. I'm going to ask you to give fealty to the judge's order, to the judge's instruction, if you would, at the end of this case, and make your decision based on whether the Government has proved its case beyond a reasonable doubt. And I'm confident that, at the conclusion of this case, you will have the doubt, and at that time, I will ask you to find HP not guilty. Thank you.

The Court: We'll now hear the evidence in the case, ladies and gentlemen.

GP: At this time, Your Honor, the Government calls MB.

(Thereupon, MB, having been called as a witness on behalf of the Government and having been first duly sworn by the deputy clerk, was examined and testified.)

Direct examination by GP:

Q. Good morning, MB. How are you?

A. Fine. Good morning.

Q. Feeling okay?

A. Yes.

Q. MB, please introduce yourself to the ladies and gentlemen of this jury by stating your name, and then I'd like for you to spell it.

A. My name is MB. It's MB.

Q. And, MB, do you go by a nickname from time to time?

A. Yes.

Q. What is it?

A. MB.

Q. Now, MB, I hate to ask you this question, but how old are you?

A. Thirty-nine.

Q. Okay. And what city did you grow up in?

A. Washington, DC.

Q. What part of the city?

A. Southeast.
Q. At some point—well, before I get there, are you married or single?
A. Single.
Q. Do you have any kids?
A. Yes.
Q. How many kids do you have?
A. Six.
Q. And do you have a son by the name of MB?
A. Yes.
Q. How old is MB now?
A. Ten.
Q. When was his birthday party?
A. On November the 7th.
Q. Was it—
A. I mean, October 7th. Sorry.
Q. I knew it better than you, didn't I? Now, I'd like to ask: Do you know an individual by the name of JH?
A. Yes.
Q. How do you know JH?
A. He's my son's cousin.
Q. Which—which son?
A. MB.
Q. Does JH go by a nickname?
A. Yes.
Q. What is that?
A. JH.
Q. And how long have you known JH?
A. For, like, two and a half years.
Q. And how would you characterize your relationship with JH?
A. It's good.
Q. At some point this year, did you live in the 1400 block of Good Hope Road?
A. Yes.
Q. And, specifically, did you live in a home located at 1435 Good Hope Road?
A. Yes.

Q. Did you live there back in April?
A. Yes.
Q. Of this year? Excuse me?
A. Yes.
Q. And who did you live there with?
A. Me and my six kids.
Q. Did you own that home?
A. Rented it.
Q. How long had you been in the home as of April of this year?
A. Seven years.
Q. From time to time, did you ever offer JH a place to stay?
A. Yes.
Q. Why did you do that?
A. Because he was a nice guy. He's my son's cousin, and at the time, he didn't have a place to go live at.
Q. Did you ever leave JH at home with your kids alone?
A. Yes.
Q. Why did you do that?
A. Because I trusted him.
Q. Let's talk about a particular—well, describe 1435 for us. What does it look like?
A. It's a brick house, a single home, with a white front door.
Q. How many bedrooms?
A. Five bedrooms.
Q. How many floors?
A. Three.
Q. And so you go in from Good Hope Road. That's the first floor?
A. Yes.
Q. Then you go up?
A. Go up the steps. And then there's—
Q. —second—
A. —a basement.
Q. And then there's a basement?
A. Yes.
Q. Do you also have an attic?
A. Yes.

Q. Did you have an attic back in April?
A. Yes.
Q. Did anyone stay in the attic at any time?
A. No, sir.
Q. And when JH would stay with you, where would he usually sleep?
A. Downstairs in the basement. I had two rooms.
Q. How often would JH stay with you?
A. From time to time.
Q. Let me show you a couple of photographs.
THE COURT: Any objection?
MM: No, Your Honor.
THE COURT: You may display them.
GP: Thank you, Your Honor.
I'm showing you first—well, you've seen this before, haven't you?
A. Yes.
Q. I'm showing you Government's 15. What is Government's 15? What does it show?
A. The front of my house.
Q. And the address is what?
A. 1435.
Q. Okay. And showing you Government's 16, what is Government's 16?
A. The front door of the entrance of the house. And that's off of—
Q. Good Hope Road?
A. Yes.
GP: Okay. I move for the admission of Government's 15 and 16.
THE COURT: Be admitted.
(Government's Exhibit Numbers 15 and 16 admitted into evidence.)
GP: All right. Back to the 27th of April of this year, Ms. Beckham, do you recall what occurred in your house about 9:00 or 10:00 a.m. that morning?
A. Yes, sir.
Q. Tell us about that.
A. That morning, I had sent my two daughters off to school. Me and my two youngest sons, which is AB and MB—
Q. How old is AB?

A. AB is thirteen now.
Q. At the time, how old was he?
A. He was twelve.
Q. All right. Go ahead.
A. Someone knocked at the front door. JH came upstairs and said, "MB, come to the door. My uncle's at the door. Tell him I'm not in here."
Q. Did he tell—did JH tell you why he wanted you to say that at that time?
A. Yes.
MM: Objection to the hearsay, Your Honor.
THE COURT: Explains the witness's subsequent actions, so it won't be offered for the truth.
GP: Go ahead.
THE COURT: You can answer.
DIRECT EXAMINATION BY GP (CONTINUED):
Q. Did JH explain to you why?
A. JH said something had occurred with his brother's dogs, which is MS, he owned at the barbershop.
Q. Okay. Now, to that point, what is on either side of your house?
A. It's the barbershop and the school next door.
Q. Okay. The school is on one side and the barbershop is on the other?
A. Yes.
Q. Do you know the name of that barbershop?
A. Cut Them Up.
Q. All right. Now, after JH explained to you—
A. They were looking out the side window as I was standing at the front door. And they said—
MM: Objection, Your Honor, to the hearsay.
THE COURT: Is it present sense impression?
GP: Yes, Your Honor.
THE COURT: I'll allow it as that.
GP: What—
THE WITNESS: They said HP walked through the side of the entrance to my basement door, which is the side door.

Q. Side—side of the house?
A. The side of the house.
Q. Could you see the side of the house where your sons were referring to at that point?
A. Yes.
Q. Okay. And where were you standing?
A. I had just shut the front door, and I went to the window.
Q. And from the window, what could you see?
A. I opened the window, and I looked out the window, and HP, he was knocking at my side door.
Q. What did that side door lead into?
A. To my basement.
Q. What else did you notice about HP?
A. I actually opened the front door. Me and AB and MB, we went back out on the front porch and looked over the banister, and HP was standing at the side door with a gun.
Q. And how—how was HP holding this gun?
A. In his hand.
Q. And how did he have the gun? Where was the gun pointed?
A. It was just straight down in his hand.
Q. Okay. At his side?
A. At his side.
Q. Okay. Did you get a good look at that gun?
A. Yes, I did.
Q. Can you describe it for us?
A. It's a black gun, and it was, like, this long (*indicating*).
Q. Okay. For the record, you just used your index fingers.
A. Yes.
Q. About that far apart?
The Court: Ten to twelve inches.
Direct examination by GP (continued):
Q. Ten to twelve inches. Is that fair to say?
A. Yes.
Q. That's from end to end?
A. Yes.
Q. Okay. What did you do as a result of seeing this gun?

A. I—I went back in the house. I went upstairs. JH was upstairs in my room. I said, "JH"—excuse me. I said, "JH, what the hell did you do?"
Q. Well, before we get there, did HP say anything?
A. Oh, yes. He said, "Is JH in there?" I said, "No." He said, "If JH comes back, tell JH I'm going to kill his ass and come to his funeral and spit on him."
Q. Did HP ultimately leave?
A. Yes, he walked off.
Q. Did the other person leave with him?
A. The other person had walked off before—he had left the porch before HP walked back toward the entrance of the sidewalk and stuff.
Q. Did you see what type of car HP was in?
A. I wasn't sure. I went back in the house.
Q. Okay. And when you went back in the house—you were explaining—you did what?
A. I went upstairs. I asked JH, "What in the hell did you do? You got people coming to my house, and my kids are in here. What did you do?" He said, "MB"—
MM: Objection to the hearsay.
The Court: Sustained.
Direct examination by GP (continued):
Q. All right. Don't tell me what JH said. What did you do after JH explained to you what he had done?
A. What did I do?
Q. Yeah.
A. I, um, went back—me and my kids—I said we were going to get something to eat. We got something to eat. Then I told my kids we were going to take a nap.
Q. Did you do that?
A. Yes, we took a nap.
Q. Now, what floor of the house is your bedroom located?
A. Upstairs.
Q. Okay. Second floor?
A. Yes.

Q. Now, did there come a time on that same day that you had an opportunity to see HP again?
A. Yes.
Q. And about what time of day was that?
A. In the afternoon.
Q. Okay. What happened?
A. Actually, I was asleep. Me and my two boys, AB and MB, we were asleep, taking a nap. And my goddaughter came upstairs, running, "Mom, Mom, get up. Two dudes are at the door for JH. They said, 'Open up the damn door, or I'm going to shoot the door in.'"
Q. What did you do?
A. I got up. I'm going down the steps, and I notice a young man in my front window—he had my window up and my curtain pulled to the side.
Q. Did you recognize who that young man was?
A. No, I didn't.
Q. What else did you see?
A. I, um, said, "I'm coming. I'm trying to get the door open." I couldn't get the door open because they had already kicked the door in, and it was jammed. I said, "I can't open the door."
Q. Now, was the door—was the door open or closed at that point?
A. It was closed at the time, but it was jammed. I couldn't open it.
Q. I see. Go ahead.
A. I said, "I can't open the door." The other young man came around and just kicked the door in.
Q. Did you see that person kick the door in?
A. Yes, I did.
Q. And how did you manage to see that?
A. Because I have a side window right by the front door.
Q. What did you do once the door was kicked in?
A. Once the door was kicked in, HP and the other guy ran in. HP was holding a gun.
Q. Was that gun familiar to you?
A. Yes, it was.
Q. How so?

A. Because I had seen it earlier that day.
Q. What happened next?
A. I ran out the front door.
Q. Why did you run out the door?
A. Because I was scared.
Q. What happened?
A. Me and AB ran out the front door, and I noticed once I got out the door, my baby wasn't with me—MB.
Q. Did you hear anything coming from inside the house?
A. Yes, I heard gunshots coming.
Q. Approximately how many?
A. Like, four or five.
Q. What happened then?
A. I started hollering, screaming, "Oh my god! Oh my god! My baby is in the house. My baby is in the house." I immediately called 911 on my cell phone.
Q. Okay. Now, have you had an opportunity to listen to that 911 call before you took the stand this morning?
A. Yes.
Q. And was that 911 call accurate?
A. Yes.
GP: If I could just have the Court's indulgence.
Direct examination by GP (continued):
Q. I'd like to play that for you, MB. Just give me a moment.
The Court: What exhibit number is this?
GP: I'm sorry, Your Honor. Number 6.
(Audio being played, not reported.)
Direct examination by GP (continued):
Q. MB, is that your voice?
A. Yes.
GP: At this time, I move in the admission of Government's Number 6, Your Honor.
The Court: Be admitted.
(Government's Exhibit Number 6 admitted into evidence.)
Direct examination by GP (continued):

Q. Now, just for clarification purposes, MB, you made that 911 call outside the house, correct?
A. Yes.
Q. Where were you standing when you made that call?
A. By the barbershop.
Q. Okay. We heard other voices in the background. Can you explain that?
A. Well, um, my son, my oldest son, JB, he was downstairs in the basement with his girlfriend. They didn't hear anything. But they came upstairs afterwards, and they were asking what happened, and I told them what happened.
Q. So that's the conversation we heard—
A. Yes.
Q. On the recording?
A. Yes.
Q. Okay. Now, when the dispatch operator asked you if you knew who it was or whether you could describe the person that did this, you said, "No," right?
A. Yes.
Q. You heard that, didn't you?
A. Yes.
Q. Can you explain why you said that?
A. At the time, I was, um—I was, um, on the run for violation of probation, and I was scared to give my name.
Q. Now, you're on probation for what?
A. Um—um, for failure to appear.
Q. Okay. And you failed to appear in connection with what kind of case?
A. Solicitation.
Q. Okay. Now, once the 911 call was made, what did you do?
A. I, um, waited until the police came.
Q. Did you see anyone exit your house?
A. Yes.
Q. Tell us about that.

A. When I was standing outside, HP and the other guy ran back down the steps and out the front door and jumped into a black truck.
Q. Now, what did you do after they left the area?
A. The police arrived.
Q. Did you tell the police what happened?
A. Yes.
Q. Did you have an opportunity to talk to the police in connection with their presentation of photographs later on that day?
A. Yes.
Q. And were you shown what is called a photo array?
A. Yes.
Q. Or photo spread?
A. Yes.
Q. Do you remember that?
A. The photo they showed me when they came into the house.
Q. And where were you shown that photo spread?
A. At my house.
Q. Now, when the police officer showed you Government's Number 10, which is the photo spread, did they suggest to you in any way which photograph to choose?
I'm showing you Government's Number 10. Take a look at that for me, MB. Do you recognize what this is?
A. No.
Q. And did you select a photograph after they asked you if you recognized anyone?
A. Yes.
Q. Which one did you select?
A. Number 8.
Q. And what did you tell the police that number 8 was responsible for doing?
A. Shooting in my house.
Q. And you recognized number 8 to be who?
A. HP.
Q. HP. Do you know his last name?
A. No, I don't.

Q. Okay. Do you see the person you pointed out in Government's Number 10A. Yes.
Q. and called HP in the courtroom?
A. Yes.
Q. Would you please look in his direction and point to him?
A. Right there.
Q. Can you describe the color of his shirt?
A. Yellow.
GP: Your Honor, may the record reflect that the witness has identified and made an in-court identification of the defendant?
THE COURT: The record will so reflect.
GP: We'd also move for the admission of Government's Number 10.
THE COURT: Number 10 will be admitted.
GP: May I publish it to the jury?
THE COURT: Yes, you may. Publish it means, ladies and gentlemen, we're going to pass them—are you going to pass them along?
GP: Yes, Your Honor.
THE COURT: We're going to pass it along. You can take a quick look as the testimony is going forward.
(Government's Exhibit Number 10 admitted into evidence.)
DIRECT EXAMINATION BY GP (CONTINUED):
Q. Could you point to number 8 for the ladies and gentlemen?
(Witness complies.)
GP: Court's indulgence. Thank you, MB. Your Honor, I have no further questions.
MM: May I? Thank you, Your Honor.
CROSS-EXAMINATION BY MM:
Q. Hello again, MB.
A. Good morning.
Q. MB, I just want to ask you: You testified that earlier that day, on April 27, there was a knock at the door, and I think you said it was JH's uncle who was at the door, correct?
A. Yes.
Q. And JH's uncle's name is DH. Is that right?
A. I don't know him.
Q. Had you ever seen him before?

A. No, I haven't.
Q. Have you ever seen him since?
A. No, I haven't.
Q. And I don't want you to tell me what anybody said, but did you have any conversations with him, the uncle, that is?
A. That morning at the door, I told him JH was not in my home.
Q. Other than that, did you have any conversations with him?
A. No, I didn't.
Q. Okay. And, MB, I want to ask you about that 911 call. The 911 call that you made, you made out on Good Hope Road right in front of Cut Them Up, right?
A. Yes.
Q. Right. And that's just, I guess, one house, even though it's not a house—it's one—it would be like one house down from your place. Is that correct?
A. Right next door.
Q. Is that before or after you say you saw these individuals leaving your house and getting into the car and leaving?
A. That was before.
Q. Okay. And—but it was after you claimed to have been able to see HP in your house. Isn't that right?
A. Can you repeat yourself?
Q. Sure. What your testimony is, is that you saw HP come into your house, and then you went out of the house. Isn't that right?
A. Right.
Q. And then you made the 911 call?
A. Yes.
Q. Correct? I want to play just a very brief clip.
MM: It is a repeat, Your Honor, but it's a very short version.
THE COURT: That's fine.
BY MM:
Q. Then I want to ask you a question about that, MB.
A. Okay.
(Audio being played, not reported.)
CROSS-EXAMINATION BY MM (CONTINUED):

Q. All right. That's on the street after you say you saw HP in your living room with a gun, right?
A. Ran through my front door with a—yes.
Q. And the last thing you told that dispatcher was, "I don't know who," correct?
A. Yes.
Q. All right. Now, let me play another clip for you. It's 0:45 to 0:51, Counsel.
(Audio being played, not reported.)
Cross-examination by MM (continued):
Q. Again, that's you talking to the dispatcher, correct?
A. Yes.
Q. And you told them you ran out the front door, and then you told them you ran out the back door, correct?
A. Yes.
Q. I'm going to play another clip, one minute to 1:06 for Counsel.
(Audio being played, not reported.)
Cross-examination by MM (continued):
Q. That's you telling the dispatcher that you didn't even know what these guys looked like, correct?
A. Yes.
Q. And again, that's out on Good Hope Road, just a few minutes after you say you witnessed HP in your house, correct?
A. Yes.
Q. 1:45 to 1:54 for Counsel.
(Audio being played, not reported.)
Cross-examination by MM (continued):
Q. And, again, that's you telling the dispatcher that you didn't see the suspects, correct?
A. I seen them.
Q. Oh. I'm asking you what you told the dispatcher. You told them that you didn't see them, correct?
A. Yes, because it happened so fast.
Q. Um-hmmm. It was real quick, right?
A. Yes.
Q. All right. Finally 2:35 to 2:45 for Counsel.

(Audio being played, not reported.)

Cross-examination by MM (continued):

Q. And—and, finally, that's you telling the dispatcher you don't know who it is. You don't know him. "I don't know, ma'am." Isn't that right?

A. Yes.

Q. Okay. At the scene, the police arrived about how long after you made that 911 call?

A. Like a minute or two.

Q. Okay. And you first talked to some uniformed police officers, correct?

A. Yes.

Q. You talked to a detective on the scene, a Detective Hollins also, right?

A. Yes.

Q. But when you talked to these uniformed police officers, you did not tell them that it was HP, correct?

A. I said I did not know, because I did not know who it was. My sons, they know HP. I don't know HP.

Q. So again, you didn't tell those uniformed police officers that it was HP. Isn't that right?

A. I told them—yes, I did tell them that it was HP because my two sons—that I witnessed HP come through the door when my—my nine-year-old son—my ten-year—excuse me. My twelve-year-old son, AB, he seen HP come through the door.

Q. Forgive me, ma'am, but I'm not allowed to ask you what other people may have seen or said. I can only ask you what you saw, correct?

A. Yes.

Q. And those uniformed police officers were asking you if you knew who it was who had run up in your house and shot up your house? They asked you that question, right?

A. Yes.

Q. And what you either saw or did. And—

A. Yes, I seen him come through the door.

Q. Yeah. I'm actually not asking you that, though. What I'm asking you is: Those uniformed police officers that you first talked to on the scene, isn't it true that you did not tell those officers that it was HP?

A. I don't remember.

Q. And in fact, the only description you gave those officers was that it was a Black male with dreads. Isn't that right?

A. Yes.

Q. Okay. And it wasn't until you spoke with Detective Hollins that you mentioned the name HP. Isn't that right?

A. Yes.

Q. Okay. And Detective Hollins showed up, like, twenty minutes later. By later, I mean about twenty minutes after you made that 911 call, correct?

A. Yes.

Q. Okay. And at the time you were talking with Detective Hollins, your son, MB, was on the first floor speaking with some of those other officers, correct?

A. I don't remember.

Q. You don't remember where MB was? Do you know whether MB was—am I saying that right? Is it MB?

A. MB.

Q. MB. Was MB—do you remember seeing him speaking with any officers?

A. Yes.

Q. Okay. And when he was speaking with the officers, was it on the first floor?

A. On the front porch.

Q. Okay. And is that where you were also, on the front porch, when you were speaking to the officers?

A. Yes. Because we were not allowed to go back into the house.

Q. Okay. So when you spoke with the—so I can be clear—when you spoke with the uniformed officers, the first officers that you spoke with, that was on the front porch, correct?

A. Yes.

Q. And later, when Detective Hollins showed up, that interview was also conducted on the front porch, correct?
A. Yes.
Q. Because they wouldn't let you go back into the house, correct?
A. Yes.
Q. And when MB was speaking to the police officers, that was on the front porch as well?
A. Yes.
Q. And could you please describe for our jury how big your front porch is?
A. It's big. It's wide. It's big. It's a nice-sized front porch.
Q. Okay. With regard to the length of—we call this the well of the court, this whole big circle here. With regard to the length of this table to the jury bench over there, would you say that's approximately the length of your porch?
A. Yes.
Q. Okay. And about how deep is it?
A. Um, from this table to about where GP is sitting.
Q. So let the record reflect you're pointing to the end of the stenographer's table, correct?
A. Yes.
Q. To the front of the table at which GP is sitting?
A. Yes.
Q. Okay. Now, I take it you could hear some of what was going on between those officers and MB, correct?
A. No, because they were talking to him on the side.
Q. Okay. They were talking to him on the side, but you were also on the porch, correct?
A. Yes, but I was sitting on the bench.
Q. Okay. You were sitting at the bench in the middle of the porch?
A. It's further over by my living room windows.
MM: May I have the Court's indulgence for a moment?
The Court: Um-hmmm.
MM: I'm going to show you what's been introduced as Government's Exhibit Number 16. May I, Your Honor?
Cross-examination by MM (continued):

Q. I'm going to hold—it's going to be a little awkward for you, because I want the jury to be able to see, so I'm going to have to hold it behind your head, so you will have to turn around a little bit. And the question I have for you is: Well, that's your front porch, right?

A. Right.

Q. Okay. And that is a wooden floor to the front porch, right?

A. Yes.

Q. Okay. And where is the bench that you're talking about?

A. It's over behind this wall right here where the window is, the front window.

Q. Okay. You mean this right here?

A. Yes.

Q. The front window. That's a pillar, not a wall, correct?

A. No. Right here where this brick wall is right here.

Q. Okay. Is there a bench over by the window?

A. I had two front windows, and there's a bench sitting up on the front porch.

Q. Did you take that bench with you when you moved?

A. No, I did not.

Q. So there's a brick wall that extends across the front of the porch, correct?

A. Yes.

Q. And there was a bench that was on the other side of this wall that I'm pointing to right now, which is on the right-hand side of the picture?

A. Yes.

Q. But it wasn't inside the building?

A. Inside the house, no, it wasn't.

Q. Okay. And on what side was MB being interviewed? What side of the porch was he being interviewed on?

A. Down the steps in front of the house.

Q. Okay. Because there are steps, and then there's a little lawn right in front of your house, correct?

A. Right, yes.

Q. Right? It's a little square, and there's another little stone wall below that, correct? And if you go over that stone, then that's a sidewalk, right?

A. Right.

Q. So he wasn't down on the sidewalk?

A. No. He was down from the steps.

Q. Okay. Is that fair to say he was within ten or fifteen feet of you?

A. I'm not sure.

Q. Okay. So while you were being interviewed—not by those original officers, not by the uniformed police officers you first spoke with, but while you were being interviewed by Detective Hollins—do you remember whether MB was still being interviewed by the police or not?

A. No, I don't.

Q. Okay. But you heard MB say the name HP. Is that right?

A. Yes, I did.

Q. And then you told Detective Hollins that it was HP, correct? I mean, you identified who the shooter was, and you told him it was HP, correct?

A. Yes.

Q. Now, your testimony, though, today is that you didn't recognize him at the time. In other words, when he first came into your house, you didn't recognize that it was HP, correct?

A. Yes.

Q. All right. You do remember testifying in front of the grand jury, don't you?

A. Yes.

Q. And you testified in front of the grand jury on May 31, 2011?

A. Yes.

Q. Page 14, 4 to 10 for Counsel.

I'm going to read something to you, and I'm going to ask you if this is what occurred at the grand jury.

Isn't it true that at the grand jury—it's 4 to 10, page 14—you were asked the following questions and gave the following answers—

GP: Objection.

The Court: Okay.

(Bench conference.)

MM: 4 to 10.

GP: It seems to me that question has not been posed to the witness to give her an opportunity to respond to the specific impeachment material. It's just an open-ended attempt to read out of the grand jury.

MM: Your Honor, specifically it—

The Court: It's inconsistent, so he has a right to confront her with the inconsistent statement.

GP: I—I just don't think the foundation has been laid for specifically what is inconsistent.

The Court: Overruled. Thank you.

(Open court.)

The Court: Overruled.

Cross-examination by MM (continued):

Q. MB, when you testified in front of the grand jury, you were under oath, just like you're under oath here. Isn't that right?

A. Yes.

Q. And you had some conversations with GP prior to going into the grand jury, correct?

A. Yes.

Q. And you understood before you went into the grand jury how important it was to tell the truth in front of the grand jury, correct?

A. Yes.

Q. And you were asked the following questions, and you gave the following answers, were you not:

Question: "Okay."

Your answer was: "And DH had the curtain open, and I happened to see a dude standing beside the window."

Question: "Did you recognize this person?"

And your answer: "At the time, I didn't, but I do now."

"Who was it?"

"His name was HP."

You were asked those questions, and you gave those answers at the grand jury. Isn't that right?

A. Yes.

Q. And you were aware, were you not, in April of 2011, when all this happened, that Jo-Jo was having a problem with HP, his cousin, weren't you?

A. No, I was not.

Q. But JH told you he was, didn't he?

A. That morning, he had told me. And he said that something had happened with the dogs.

Q. So he told you that his dog Eve had attacked the dog that belonged to HP's family, correct?

A. He said MS's dogs.

Q. Oh, MS's dogs?

A. Yes.

Q. And he told you that he thought HP was mad about that, correct?

A. Excuse me?

Q. He told you that he thought that HP would be angry with him because of that, correct?

A. Yes.

Q. And that was that morning before all of this happened, correct?

A. Yes.

Q. Now, when you say you saw HP come up to the door with the gun, at the time when the door was kicked in, did you see HP with the gun?

A. When I saw HP with the gun, I was standing at the little window right by the front door. The other guy, he had lifted the window in the living room up. And that window had a curtain, so I pulled the curtain back, and that's when I saw HP standing right in front of that window.

Q. I'm going to show you Government's Exhibit Number 16 again and ask you if you can point to the jury which of the windows you're talking about. First of all, is that window in this picture?

A. Yes, it is.

Q. Again, I'm going to hold it behind you. It's a little uncomfortable, but I have to do it.

A. It's this window right here. I was looking out this window. HP was on the side right here, and the guy—he was at the window, and the door was jammed, already kicked in.
Q. I'm going to stop and ask you, because we can't see it in this picture—there's no window on that particular door, correct?
A. There's a window right here.
Q. Yes. But I mean on the door itself. The thing that swings back and forth; in other words, it's not a glass door?
A. No.
Q. Okay. So it's a steel door, correct?
A. Yes.
Q. And your testimony is that you came all the way up to the door but didn't go through it. You were on the other side of this window looking through, correct?
A. Yes, I was.
Q. Okay, now, you do remember speaking with Detective Hollins, correct?
A. Yes.
Q. And you do remember telling Detective Hollins that you never made it to the door; that you were on the stairs when the door got kicked in? Do you remember telling him that?
A. No, I don't.
Q. Is it possible that you told him that?
A. I don't remember.
Q. And when this person came in with the gun, what was the person doing with the gun?
A. Had it to his side and ran straight up the steps.
Q. Okay, and this person didn't point the gun at you, right?
A. No, sir.
Q. But you did tell Officer Smith and Detective Hollins that this person put the gun in your face?
A. No, I did not.
Q. So you didn't say that?
A. No, I did not.
Q. And you say you heard how many shots?
A. About four or five.

Q. And do you remember telling Detective Hollins that you only heard two?
A. No, I did not.
Q. No, you don't remember, or no, you didn't tell him?
A. I don't remember.
Q. Now, after this happened, did you go back in the house?
A. Um—
Q. Let me—that's unfair. I want to point you to a specific period of time. After you go outside, after you make the 911 call, but before the police arrived, did you go back in the house?
A. No, I did not, because my nine-year-old son had run down the steps and came out the door.
Q. And that's MB?
A. Yes.
Q. Okay, and so Maurice was there waiting, just like you were, for the police to show up, correct?
A. Yes.
Q. All right, and I take it you talked to Maurice about what happened, tried to comfort him?
A. Yes.
Q. And did you tell him what happened?
A. No, um—
Q. Again, I have to tell you, I'm not allowed to ask you what anybody said, but I am going to ask you whether you told him what you had witnessed?
A. Did I tell MB?
Q. Yeah, MB.
A. No, I did not.
Q. Now—you did testify that while you were making the 911 call, JB came up from the basement and came outside, correct?
A. Yes.
Q. And JB is your son as well, correct?
A. Yes.
Q. How old is JB?
A. JB is eighteen.

Q. Okay. And we actually heard that exchange in the background on the 911 call, correct?
A. Yes.
Q. When you were explaining to JB, very excitedly, admittedly—but explained to JB what happened, correct?
A. Yes.
Q. All right. And nowhere in that 911 call did you say, "HP just came in and shot up our house." Isn't that right?
A. No, I did not.
Q. Um-hmm. Now, when the police interviewed you, you did give them an incorrect name, correct?
A. I gave them—excuse me? Say that again.
Q. You gave them an incorrect name. In other words—
A. Yes, my—yes.
Q. Okay. Because you were worried about your warrants?
A. Yes.
Q. And you have a prior conviction for solicitation in 2009, correct?
A. Yes.
Q. And you also have a BRA, correct?
A. Yes.
Q. And a BRA is a charge for failing to show up in court, isn't that correct?
A. Yes.
Q. And those were both prosecuted by the US Attorney's Office, correct?
A. Yes.
Q. The same office that GP works for, correct?
A. I guess. I don't know.
The Court: Ladies and gentlemen, you've heard evidence that the witness has a previous conviction. You may consider the previous conviction in evaluating the witness's credibility.
MM: Thank you, ma'am.
GP: Thank you, Your Honor.
Redirect examination by GP:
Q. MB, how close were you standing when HP ran into your house?

A. I was standing right by that little window when they came in. I ran right out the door.
Q. All right. So if I can represent HP, tell me when to stop as I walk backwards to represent how far you were from him when he came into your house.
A. About right there—
Q. Closer or further?
A. Um, about right there.
Q. About right here?
A. Um-hmm.
The Court: Six feet—five, six feet.
Redirect examination by GP (continued):
Q. And from five or six feet away from HP, did you get a look at his face?
A. Yes.
Q. Did he look in your direction?
A. I don't remember.
Q. How is it that you had a chance to look at his face?
A. Because when I opened the curtain of the window, I saw his face.
Q. Is that the same face you see sitting at the Counsel's table?
A. Yes.
Q. Now, Counsel made an issue about your 911 call and your inability to describe who the perpetrator was. You heard that, right?
A. Yes.
Q. You answered those questions, right?
A. Yes.
Q. Did you know, at the time HP came into your house, his name?
A. No, I did not.
Q. How well did you know HP at all?
A. I don't know him. I know him by seeing him coming up and down Good Hope Road at times.
Q. Had you ever had any social dealings with HP?
A. No, I have not.
Q. Had HP ever visited your home?
A. No, he had not.

Q. You mentioned during cross-examination that your sons knew HP more than you did?
A. Yes.
Q. Can you explain that?
A. Well, they're kids, and they're from the neighborhood, so they pretty much know the people from the neighborhood, the guys.
Q. Is there any family relationship between MB and HP?
A. Well, yes, because MB's father is supposed to be his cousin.
Q. Okay. So it's safe to say that MB knows HP better than you do?
A. Yes.
Q. Now, you were interviewed on the front porch, correct?
A. Yes.
Q. And Counsel asked you how much distance between where you were being interviewed and where MB was being interviewed. Is that correct?
A. Yes.
Q. During the interview, were you able to hear both the questions from the police officers and the answers from MB?
A. No.
Q. And when you heard the name HP, in what context did you hear that? In other words, did you hear the question before you heard MB say HP?
A. No. MB said it was HP because he saw him earlier that morning.
Q. Okay. So you heard MB say that to the police?
A. Yes. And MB saw when HP—
MM: Objection, Your Honor.
Redirect examination by GP (continued):
Q. Okay. You don't have to tell me what MB said. Is what MB said the reason you then provided information as to HP's involvement?
A. Yes.
Q. Did you only provide that information based upon what MB said or what you believed to be true?
A. What I believed to be true.
Q. Did you actually see HP enter the house, or did you rely only on what MB told you?
A. I actually saw him enter the house.

Q. Why didn't you tell the police when they first arrived at your house that it was HP who was responsible for this? Why didn't you just tell them, "Officers, it was HP"?
A. Because I didn't know at the time, until my son said that it was HP. He said his name.
Q. All right.
A. And I didn't know the name.
Q. Let's understand what you're saying. Are you saying you didn't know HP's name as of April 27, is that correct?
A. Yes.
Q. Did you remember what he looked like as of April 27 when he left the house?
A. Yes.
Q. Did you have an independent recollection of what he looked like?
A. Yes.
Q. And was it your independent recollection that caused you to identify HP?
A. Yes.
MM: Objection to the leading at this point, Your Honor.
The Court: Overruled. It's a summary of what has been established.
Redirect examination by GP (continued):
Q. You had a prior conviction, correct?
A. Yes.
Q. And you completed whatever obligations you had in connection with that case, correct?
A. Yes.
Q. Now, has the Government, including myself or police officers, any member of the United States Attorney's Office, provided you any promise in connection with your prior cases in exchange for your testimony today?
A. No.
GP: I have nothing further, Your Honor.
The Court: Thank you, ma'am. You may step down.
(Witness excused.)
MM: May we approach briefly, Your Honor?
The Court: Uh-huh.

(Bench conference.)

MM: I just ask that this particular witness remain available, Your Honor.

The Court: Can you arrange that?

GP: Yes.

The Court: Do you need a break or—I'm stopping at 1:00.

The Court Reporter: That's fine.

The Court: Okay. I'll ask the jury.

(Open court.)

The Court: Okay, ladies and gentlemen, I do plan on going until 1:00. Does anybody need a break at this point? Okay, ladies and gentlemen, we'll take a short recess. Do not discuss the case among yourselves or with anyone else. Again, step into the jury room for about ten minutes. Thank you.

(Jury out.)

The Court: Who is next?

GP: MB.

The Court: Okay. We'll start his testimony. Thank you.

GP: Thank you.

(Brief recess.)

The Deputy Clerk: Recalling from Your Honor's trial calendar, *United States v. HP*, Case Number 2011-CF3-8205.

GP: GP for the United States.

MM: MM for HP.

The Court: GP?

GP: A sergeant here, Your Honor, made an observation as he was standing outside the courtroom. He passed that observation on to me. And what he said was he saw a gentleman who came out of the courtroom wearing a red garment. I did not observe the individual, but he said that he saw this individual exit the courtroom and then stop, turn, and stare at young MB, which appeared to the sergeant to be an attempt to intimidate the young man.

MM: May I have just a second, Your Honor? The defendant's brother has been here, Your Honor. I don't remember whether he was wearing red or not.

THE COURT: I don't know, either.

MM: But I would certainly volunteer to speak with MP, his brother.

THE COURT: Well, let me ask GP. I'm prepared to have MM handle it that way unless you have another suggestion.

GP: Well, we would ask that he not be permitted in the courtroom during MB's testimony.

MM: If it was a more clear case of an attempt to intimidate, I would agree, Your Honor. But from what I've heard described—

THE COURT: No. I'm going to order it, if that individual—the brother—is wearing red.

MM: I don't remember. Shall I step out and find out?

THE SERGEANT: I can identify the person I saw come out of the courtroom. Yes, sir.

GP: Can we bring him in, Your Honor?

THE COURT: Sure.

MM: As the Court knows, this next witness is the one where the defense is reserving the right to reopen cross should that be necessary, Your Honor.

THE COURT: Thank you. I'm prepared to get started at this point, unless—

GP: It's a red undergarment.

THE COURT: You're saying that's the individual?

THE SERGEANT: Yes, sir.

THE COURT: Do you want to go talk to him?

MM: Yes, Your Honor. That is the defendant's brother, MP, Your Honor. He tells me he did see little MB, and he said he just looked at him and then walked past.

THE COURT: Okay. Well, I obviously can't have a mini hearing about this. I think it's appropriate at this time just to ask him to step out during the course of this one witness. Other family members here are watching the trial.

GP: Thank you, Your Honor.

THE COURT: Ready for the jury.

(Jury in.)

GP: The Government calls MB, Your Honor.

(Thereupon, MB, having been called as a witness on behalf of the Government and having been first duly sworn by the deputy clerk, was examined and testified.)

THE COURT: And can I just ask you to keep your voice up, sir.

THE WITNESS: Yes.

THE COURT: Thank you.

DIRECT EXAMINATION BY GP:

Q. MB, you see that microphone in front of you?
A. Yes, ma'am.
Q. Talk to that microphone, okay, so everybody in this room can hear what MB has to say, okay? You have to say yes. Tell me yes.
A. Yes.
Q. Thank you. MB?
A. Yes.
Q. See these ladies and gentlemen over here?
A. Yes, ma'am.
Q. Are you calling me ma'am?
A. No.
Q. Okay. What do you mean to say?
A. Yes.
Q. Thank you. All right. MB, you see these nice people over here?
A. Yes.
Q. They're going to smile, and they're going to be nice to you, okay?
A. Yes.
Q. All right. So nothing to worry about, okay?
A. Yes.
Q. All right. MB, you know how to spell your name, don't you?
A. Yes.
Q. What I'd like you to do, MB, is tell these nice people what your first name is and what your last name is right now, okay?
A. Yes.
Q. Go ahead.
A. MB.
Q. Spell MB for us.
A. MB.
Q. Great. And can you spell MB?

A. Yes.
Q. Go ahead.
A. MB.
Q. All right. Excellent. MB, you go to school, of course, right?
A. Yes.
Q. What school do you go to?
A. Wheaton.
Q. Okay. And what grade are you in?
A. Fifth.
Q. And what is your favorite subject in school?
A. Math.
Q. Are you good at it?
A. Yes.
Q. Bring good grades home?
A. Yes.
Q. All right, fantastic. MB, you and I have had a chance to talk about why you're here today, haven't we?
A. Yes.
Q. And I told you that the most important thing for you to do is to—what? What did I tell you to always do?
A. Tell the truth.
Q. Okay. Now, MB, do you know the difference between telling the truth and telling a lie?
A. Yes.
Q. Okay. If I—excuse me—if I were to say to you, MB, that this suit I'm wearing was white, would that be the truth, or would that be a lie?
A. A lie.
Q. Okay. And if I were to tell you that this suit was gray, would that be the truth, or would that be a lie?
A. The truth.
Q. Okay. Now, you have rules at home, correct?
A. Yes.
Q. And your mom tells you what to do which is right and what not to do that's wrong, correct?
A. Yes.

Q. What does your mom tell you about telling lies?

MM: Objection, Your Honor, to what his mom tells him.

The Court: What does he understand?

GP: Yes.

The Court: And what does he understand about telling lies?

Direct examination by GP (continued):

Q. What do you understand about whether a lie is good or not?

A. It's not good.

Q. Okay. It's always better to do what?

A. Tell the truth.

Q. That's exactly what you're going to do today, correct?

A. Yes.

GP: All right. Your Honor, this may be a good time.

The Court: Ladies and gentlemen, we just wanted to get through those preliminary matters. We are going to take a luncheon recess now. I told the lawyers I had a hard break meeting at 1:00, which I have to attend. So we'll take a luncheon recess now. Please be back to the jury room at 2:15. 2:15. Do not discuss the case among yourselves, or with anyone else.

Can they go in the back now, the jurors, the back entrance, C Street?

The Deputy Clerk: They should be able to, yes.

The Court: Okay. So you can go in the C Street entrance, which is near the museum. Just indicate to the CSO, the court security officers, that you're sitting jurors. Always have your badge. And you can come in that way. Sometimes at lunch, the front entrance is as busy as it is in the morning because everybody is trying to get in between 2:00 and 2:15. Enjoy your lunch. C Street.

(Jury out.)

GP: May MB be excused, Your Honor?

The Court: Thank you. MB, you may step down for lunch.

(Lunch recess.)

The Deputy Clerk: *United States v. HP*, Case Number 2011-CF3-8205.

MM: MM for HP, Your Honor.

GP: Good afternoon, Your Honor. GP for the United States.

THE COURT: Okay. On our preliminary matter, I did listen to the 911 call. And I guess I'll hear from GP. The beginning of the call is pretty straightforward, an ID. And I didn't time it, but I can't give you the exact time. I would say the first minute or so, there's a description and an ID, and maybe up to the point where the caller indicates the address of HP. Beyond that point, it just sounds like a police interview. I'm not inclined to allow it in as part of the identification.

So it's really just sort of an interview about that. They're hating, and, you know—

GP: That's fine, Judge.

THE COURT: Okay. So I don't know if this is not this witness?

GP: No. It will be the next witness, however.

THE COURT: Okay. Well, maybe what we'll do is take a break between then and see if you two can agree upon the cutoff time of the call. I've given you some general guidance.

GP: There are two calls.

THE COURT: Right. The first call is fine. I'm fine with the first call. I didn't think MM had a problem with the first call. I'm talking about the second call, about seven minutes.

GP: That's right.

THE COURT: I'm estimating about the first minute or so would be appropriate where there is an identification.

MM: I didn't time it either, but my recollection was in the beginning of the call, he said HP just shot at JH.

THE COURT: Well, I'm just—

MM: But after that, I have a problem.

THE COURT: Well, he says something about a cousin. It happened about twenty minutes ago, doesn't want to be interviewed, and then he gives an address for HP of 1362—

MM: Valley.

THE COURT: Valley Street. I think that could be part of the identification.

MM: I think that is part of the identification.

THE COURT: But beyond that—I mean, I've listened to it, and it's just as if a police officer were interviewing the witness.

GP: Very well, Your Honor.

The Court: Okay. So maybe I'll give you this back, and you can figure out exactly how far you want to go with that guidance.

GP: Thank you.

The Court: Briefly—oh, no, the jury is not back yet.

(Jury in.)

Direct examination by GP (continued):

Q. MB, good afternoon.
A. Good afternoon.
Q. MB, I don't know if I asked you, but how old are you?
A. Ten.
Q. When's your birthday?
A. October 7.
Q. Just last week, huh?
A. Yes.
Q. Happy birthday.
A. Thank you.
Q. MB, you were at home a while ago when a pretty scary thing happened inside your house, weren't you?
A. Yes.
Q. And do you remember what street you lived on when that thing happened in your house?
A. Yes.
Q. What street did you live on?
A. Good Hope.
Q. And do you know the address where you lived on Good Hope?
A. Yes.
Q. What is the address?
A. 1435.
Q. Who did you live there with?
A. My mother and my sisters and brothers.
Q. Now, I want you to think about that day that I'm talking about, okay?
A. Yes.

Q. And what I want you to do is tell the nice ladies and gentlemen what happened on that day in the morning. Do you remember what happened in the morning?
A. Yes.
Q. Okay. I only want you to tell the truth, okay?
A. Yes.
Q. All right. Go ahead and tell us what happened in the morning.
A. A man came to our house and knocked on the door and asked if JH was there, and my mother said no. Then that's when he went to the side door and had a gun, and we looked over.
Q. Okay. Now, you said he went to the side door?
A. Yes.
Q. Okay. What's that side door to?
A. To the basement.
Q. Okay. And where were you when you saw this man, MB?
A. On the front porch.
Q. Okay. And how was this man holding the gun that you saw?
A. In his hand.
Q. Do you remember what color that gun was?
A. Yes.
Q. What color was it, MB?
A. Black.
Q. Did you hear that man say anything, MB?
A. Yes.
Q. What did you hear him say, MB?
A. He was going to kill JH.
Q. Did he say anything else?
A. No.
Q. Now, did that man leave?
A. Yes.
Q. Did you see that man again later on that same day?
A. Yes.
Q. Tell us about that, MB.
A. I woke up. Then I heard a gunshot go off. Then I put the covers back over my head. Then I saw two men running downstairs—

THE COURT: Just slow down a little, MB. Just slow down a little, okay?
THE WITNESS: Yes.
THE COURT: Thank you.
DIRECT EXAMINATION BY GP (CONTINUED):
Q. Okay. Let's start again, MB. You heard two gunshots?
A. I heard one.
Q. You heard one, okay. What did you do when you heard that gunshot?
A. Put the covers back over my head.
Q. Okay. Where were you sleeping in the house?
A. In my mother's room.
Q. And what floor is your mother's room on? If you go into your house from Good Hope, do you have to go up the stairs?
A. Yes.
Q. Okay. And when you heard that gunshot and you covered your head, what do you remember happening next?
A. I took the covers off, then I saw two men run downstairs.
Q. Okay. Where were these men when you saw them, MB?
A. By the stairway.
Q. Okay. And you were still in bed when you saw them?
A. Yes.
Q. Did you get a look at their faces?
A. Yes.
Q. Did you recognize one of the persons?
A. Yes.
Q. Who was that person?
A. HP.
Q. And who was the person that you saw that morning at the side of the house holding the gun?
A. HP.
Q. How do you know HP?
A. Because I always see him around the neighborhood.
Q. So you knew what he looked like?
A. Yes.
Q. Now, did you notice any clothes that he was wearing?

A. I saw some purple shorts. I don't remember what shirt he had on.
Q. Purple shorts?
A. Yes.
Q. Now, did you actually see HP leave the house?
A. No.
Q. Did you know what kind of car he got in and left?
A. A black truck.
Q. Did you see the black truck?
A. Yes.
Q. How did you have a chance to see the black truck if you were in your mom's bedroom?
A. Because earlier that day he had a black truck.
Q. Okay. And when you say earlier that day, you mean when you saw the gun?
A. Uh-huh.
Q. Okay. Now, when you saw the black truck, where was it?
A. Parked out front of our house.
Q. Okay. Had you ever seen that black truck before?
A. Yes.
Q. Okay. And who did you see inside that black truck before?
A. HP.
Q. Now, after HP left your house, did police officers come by and show you some pictures?
A. Yes.
Q. Okay. And you had a chance to point at one of those pictures and tell the police officers what that man did, didn't you?
A. Yes.
Q. Okay, MB. I want to show you some pictures, okay?
A. Yes.
Q. All right. And we call this Government's Number 10, okay, MB?
A. Yes.
Q. Have you seen that group of pictures before, MB?
A. Yes.
Q. Okay. Is that the same group of photographs or pictures that the police officers showed you?
A. Yes.

Q. Okay. And did you point to a man in those pictures?
A. Yes.
Q. Do you see the numbers on those pictures—
A. Yes.
Q. —MB? Okay. There's 1, 2, 3, 4, 5, 6, 7, 8, and 9. Is that right?
A. Yes.
Q. Which number did you point to?
A. Number 8.
Q. Okay. Now, let's hold this up so the nice people in the jury can see it, and look my way, MB. Point to number 8 for us.
A. Okay.
Q. Who is number 8?
A. HP.
Q. And what did HP do?
A. Came in my house and shot it up.
Q. Do you see HP in this courtroom—
A. Yes.
Q. —today?
A. Yeah.
Q. Look in his direction for me, MB, okay?
(Witness complies.)
Q. All right, very good. Now, what color shirt is he wearing?
Q. A yellow shirt.
GP: Your Honor, may the record reflect that MB has made an in-court identification of the defendant.
The Court: Record will so reflect.
Direct examination by GP (continued):
Q. Now, did any police officers tell you who to choose in those pictures, MB?
A. No, sir.
Q. And are you telling the truth today, MB?
A. Yes, sir.
GP: Thank you, MB. I have no further questions.
MM: Thank you, Your Honor.
Cross-examination by MM:
Q. Hello, MB.

A. Hi.
Q. MB, did you ever meet me before today?
A. No.
Q. Well, my name is MM.
A. Yes, sir.
Q. Did you ever play the video game *Madden Football*?
A. Yes.
Q. Well, it's the same name except it's me. You just had your tenth birthday?
A. Yes.
Q. What did you get?
A. I got a happy birthday card from my family members.
Q. Nice. That's very nice. And what grade are you in now?
A. Fifth.
Q. You're in fifth grade?
A. Yes, sir.
Q. How do you like school?
A. Good.
Q. You like it good. What is your favorite class?
A. Math.
Q. Math, all right. MB, I'm going to ask you—just like GP asked you—I'm going to ask you some questions, too. Would that be okay?
A. Yes, sir.
Q. Okay. First, I just want to ask you some easy ones, like JH—you know who JH is, right?
A. Yes.
Q. And how long have you known JH?
A. For about two and a half years.
Q. And when you were living over on Good Hope Road, JH was living with you and your mom, correct?
A. No.
Q. He wasn't—he wasn't living with you and your mom at Good Hope Road?
A. No.
Q. Was he ever staying there?

A. He probably would spend the night.
Q. Okay. And you know this guy right to my right, correct? The guy with the yellow shirt, right?
A. Yes.
Q. And who is that?
A. HP.
Q. All right. And GP asked you a bunch of questions about when your house got shot up. I'm going to ask you some of those questions, too, if that's all right.
A. Yes.
Q. Okay. The day that your house got shot up—you already knew who HP was, correct?
A. Yes, sir.
Q. Okay. You'd seen him—you don't have to call me sir. You had seen him around the neighborhood lots of times, correct?
A. Yes.
Q. Okay. And are you related to HP?
A. Some people say it, but I don't really know.
Q. Okay. How about JH? Are you related to JH?
A. Yes.
Q. Okay. And do you know if JH and HP are?
A. Yes.
Q. They're cousins, right?
A. Yes.
Q. Okay. And, again, back to that day, when the house got shot up, you had seen HP a bunch of times in a black truck, correct?
A. Yes.
Q. Okay. And I think you said you saw him that day in purple shorts, right?
A. Yes.
Q. You had seen HP a bunch of times wearing purple, correct?
A. Yes.
Q. In fact, most of the times you saw HP, he was wearing the color purple. Is that right?
A. No. I only saw him sometimes wearing purple.

Q. Okay. I don't want to put any words in your mouth. Do you know what it means to put words in somebody's mouth?
A. Yes.
Q. All right. Well, I don't want to do that to you. If I ever suggest something and it's not true, don't—don't say it's true just because it will make me happy, okay?
A. Yes.
Q. Give me the straight deal, all right?
A. Yes.
Q. Okay. Now, that day, again, when the house got shot up, were you aware that HP and JH were having a beef over this dog thing?
A. Yes.
Q. Okay. And, in fact, you had overheard JH talking to your mom about it, right?
A. I wasn't in the room then.
Q. But did you hear them talking about it?
A. They told me afterwards.
Q. Okay. Afterwards, meaning after everything happened?
A. No. After they got finished talking.
Q. Oh, after they got finished talking. All right. And it was your mom and JH who were talking about the beef over the dog?
A. Yes.
Q. Okay. And at that time, did you have an understanding—I mean, were you aware of what happened with the dog?
GP: Objection.
THE WITNESS: No.
THE COURT: Overruled.
CROSS-EXAMINATION BY MM (CONTINUED):
Q. Okay. But at that time—and by that, I mean that morning before your house got shot up—you knew because of what they told you that JH didn't want to talk to HP that day, correct?
A. Yes.
Q. Okay. And now you said—when you saw HP come by in the morning—you said you were out on the porch. Is that right?
A. Yes.
Q. Okay. And you said you saw the black truck out front, correct?

A. Yes.
Q. And that was the same truck you saw before, correct?
A. Yes.
Q. And you went back upstairs and went to bed at some point in the middle of the day, around noon, correct?
A. When my mother—we had eaten, and she was like, "Come on, let's take a nap."
Q. Okay. So you weren't in school that day?
A. No.
Q. Okay. And you heard a shot, and that's what woke you up, correct?
A. Yes.
Q. And then you said you put your head back under the covers, right?
A. Yes.
Q. But I think you said that you peeked out from under the covers. Is that right?
A. No. I woke up, and then I took the covers over my head. Then I saw two men running downstairs. Then I put them back over my head.
Q. Okay. I want to ask you some questions about that, if that's okay. You were in bed when you saw these two men, right?
A. Um-hmm.
Q. And was your mother's—you were in your mother's room, right?
A. Yes.
Q. And your mother's room is— in other words, the windows of your mother's room look out on the front of the house, isn't that right?
A. No.
Q. That's the back of the house?
A. Yes.
Q. Okay. The door to your mother's bedroom faces into the hallway?
A. Yes.
Q. Okay. Was that door open or closed?
A. It was open.
Q. I want you to think hard whether it was open all the way, halfway, or how open it was.

A. It was open all the way.
Q. Okay. But these two men who came by, they were running, right?
A. Yes.
Q. Okay. And they ran past the door, correct?
A. Yes, and went down the stairway.
Q. And then went down the stairway. Now, did you know who the other person was?
A. No.
Q. Which guy came by first, the guy who you think you knew or the guy who you didn't know?
A. The guy I think I knew.
Q. Okay. And how fast were they running?
A. I don't know. They were just running.
Q. And, um, you stayed in your bedroom, isn't that correct? I'm sorry, you stayed in your mom's room, right?
A. While they ran downstairs?
Q. Yeah. After they ran downstairs?
A. I waited for like two minutes, then got up.
Q. Okay. And did JH come into the room?
A. Yes.
Q. Okay. And JH came into the room before you left the room, right?
A. Um-hmm.
Q. And you were still under the covers when JH came in, correct?
A. No.
Q. No?
A. I was sitting up.
Q. And you asked JH if he was okay, right?
A. Yes.
Q. And he told you, "I'm okay," right?
A. Uh-huh.
Q. And where did you go after that?
A. I went downstairs to my mama.
Q. Okay. And where was your mom?
A. On the porch.
Q. So your mom wasn't out on the sidewalk in front of the barbershop?

A. Yes. First, she was on the porch, then she went to by the barbershop to ask for help.
Q. Okay. So when you first went out, your mom was on the porch?
A. Yeah.
Q. And then she went in front of the barbershop?
A. Yes.
Q. All right. Did you go with her to the front of the barbershop?
A. No.
Q. All right. When you first got on the porch, did you see your mom on the phone?
A. Yes.
Q. Okay. And when you got out there, the guys who had run out of your house—you did not see them out there, right?
A. Yes.
Q. Okay. Forgive me for asking—when you say yes, you mean I'm correct; you did not see them?
A. I didn't see them drive off.
Q. You didn't see them drive off?
(Nods.)
Q. Okay. Do you remember speaking with a lady by the name of MK?
A. Yes.
Q. Okay. And you spoke with her sometime in the early part of June, about two or three weeks after this happened?
A. Yes.
Q. All right. Do you remember telling—well, first off, do you know why you went to speak with MK?
A. No.
Q. But they told you that you had to go talk to her?
A. They told me we were going, that I had to go talk to her.
Q. Okay. And you went into a little room, and it was just you and MK, correct?
A. Yes.
Q. All right. Was she a pretty nice lady?
A. Yes.

Q. Okay. And do you remember telling her that after you heard these shots, you ran downstairs and saw the black truck pulling away? Do you remember telling her that?
A. Yes.
Q. Okay. And that wasn't correct, right?
A. No.
Q. Okay. And you also told her that after you heard the shots and you ran downstairs, you told her that HP was driving the black truck away. Isn't that right?
A. Yes.
Q. And that wasn't correct, either?
A. My mother told me that.
Q. Okay. Your mom told you that. All right. Well, let me ask you some questions about that. When you got downstairs and you saw your mom on the porch, did you talk to your mom?
A. Yes.
Q. Did she—I don't want you to tell me what she said, but did she tell you what happened?
A. Yes.
Q. And did she mention the name HP?
A. No.
Q. Who else was out there on the porch when you got out there?
A. It was a lot of people. I don't remember.
Q. Are you able to estimate for the Court how many people? By that I mean, are you able to say whether it was around ten or around twenty or around thirty or anything like that?
GP: Objection. Relevance.
The Court: Overruled.
Cross-examination by MM (continued):
Q. Okay. Was there anybody out there that you knew, other than your mom, of course?
A. Yes.
Q. All right. Who was out there that you knew?
GP: Objection.
The Court: Overruled.
The Witness: My brother.

Cross-examination by MM (continued):
Q. That's JB, right?
A. Yes.
Q. All right. And who else?
A. My sister.
Q. And your sister is JB?
A. No.
Q. AB?
A. No.
Q. What's your sister's name?
A. JB.
Q. JB—is that short for JB?
A. Yes.
Q. Oh, okay. I'm asking you again about running out onto the porch, all right, when you talked to your mom. Do you remember how long you talked to your mom?
A. No.
Q. All right. Do you remember how long it was before the police came?
A. No.
Q. Okay. When these guys ran past the room, do you know where they were coming from?
A. The attic.
Q. All right. But you wouldn't have been able to see them come down from the attic from your mom's room, right?
A. No.
Q. Okay. So you heard someone on some steps, is that right?
A. Yes, because they're wooden.
Q. Now, when these two guys came by the room, only one of them had a gun. Is that right?
A. I don't remember.
Q. All right. Again, I have to ask you about MK. You remember talking to her, right?
A. Yes.
Q. Do you remember telling MK that both of them had a gun?
A. Yes.

Q. All right. But you don't remember whether both of them had a gun, do you?
A. Uh-uh. But at first, I did.
Q. All right. Well, I want to ask you about the police who showed up. The first police officers had uniforms on, correct?
A. Yes.
Q. And then there was another police officer who came, but he was in a suit like me, right?
A. I don't remember.
Q. Okay. Well, let me ask you about those police officers in uniform. When they came, they talked to you, right?
A. First, they talked to my mom.
Q. Okay. And then they talked to you?
A. Yes.
Q. All right. And when they were talking to you, where was that?
A. In the dining room.
Q. All right. I want to show you what's been marked and admitted as Government's Exhibit Number 16. MB, I'm going to come over there, if that's okay, and I'm going to hold the picture up. And I'm going to hold it behind you, so you're going to have to turn around to look at it because I want everybody to see. Could you tell the jury what that is?
A. My front door.
Q. All right. That's not your front door now, but that was your front door when you used to live on Good Hope Road, correct?
A. Yes.
Q. Okay. And when you first walked through that door in that house, what room is that?
A. That's just the hallway.
Q. Just the hallway. And what's the first room you run into when you walk in?
A. The—I mean, the living room.
Q. All right. And then there's a dining room after that, right?
A. Yes.
Q. Okay. Do you know, out here in front of the house after you walk down the steps, is there a little lawn?

A. Huh?
Q. Is there a little lawn, like a little patch of grass when you walk out of the house and go down the steps?
A. On the sides?
Q. Yeah. Kind of on the side?
A. I don't remember.
Q. All right. Well, when the police were interviewing you, were they talking to you inside or outside?
A. Outside.
Q. You said they were talking to you inside, didn't you?
A. On the outside.
Q. In other words, was it inside or outside?
A. Inside and outside.
Q. And where were they talking?
A. Inside.
Q. Inside. And were you inside, too?
A. No.
Q. Where were you when they were talking to your mom?
A. On the front porch with my brother.
Q. Okay. And that's the officers in uniforms we're talking about, right?
A. Yes.
Q. Do you remember or do you know whether a police officer who wasn't wearing a uniform ever talked to your mom?
A. No.
Q. Okay. Now, what you're saying is you were in bed the whole time when these guys were running past the room, correct?
A. Yes.
Q. All right. But when you were talking to the police officers, did you tell them that you actually ran into these guys in the hallway?
A. No.
Q. But you did tell them that only one of those guys had a gun, right?
GP: Objection.
The Witness: I don't remember.
The Court: Overruled.
Cross-examination by MM (continued):

Q. Do you remember telling the police that you didn't know whether these guys came from the attic or not?
A. Yeah. I did tell them that they came from the attic.
Q. And when the police talked to you, you told them the name HP, right?
A. Yes.
Q. Okay. But you did not tell them that HP had come by earlier, is that right?
A. Yes, I did tell them.
Q. Yes, you did tell them? That's the police—I want to be clear about what I'm talking about. The police officers in uniform who talked to you when they first came to the house, did you tell them that HP had come by earlier?
A. When they asked me.
Q. When did they ask you?
A. When they drove up and finished talking to my mom.
Q. Okay.
MM: Can I have the Court's indulgence for a moment, Your Honor? I'm about finished.
The Court: Um-hmm.
Cross-examination by MM (continued):
Q. MB, do you know if your mom knew HP?
A. No.
Q. No, you don't know or—
(Nods.)
Q. Okay. Did HP ever come over to your house on Good Hope Road?
A. No.
Q. Where would you usually see him?
A. On Valley Place.
Q. And that's not too far from where you used to live on Good Hope Road, right?
A. No.
Q. It's a couple of blocks?
A. Yes.
MM: Thank you, young man.

The Court: Okay.

GP: MB, I have no further questions. Thank you.

The Court: Thank you, MB. You may step down.

You needed a break before the next witness?

GP: Yes, Your Honor.

The Court: Okay. Ladies and gentlemen, we're going to take a break right now. The lawyers have to consult on something before the next witness. We'll try to make it go a little smoother. During the course of the recess, do not discuss the case among yourselves or with anyone else. It should be about ten minutes. Thank you.

(Jury out.)

(Brief recess.)

(Jury in.)

GP: Government calls JH, Your Honor.

The Court: Okay.

GP: Mr. Harris, good afternoon.

(Thereupon, JH, having been called as a witness on behalf of the Government and having been first duly sworn by the deputy clerk, was examined and testified.)

The Court: Ladies and gentlemen, you can see JH is in detention. The security protocol that we're undertaking in this case is no different from any other case in the courthouse, and it's not specific to JH. This is what would happen in any case in which a witness is brought from detention.

Direct examination by GP:

Q. JH, I was eager to say hello to you. I haven't seen you in a while. How are you doing this afternoon?

A. Fine.

Q. Good. JH, introduce yourself to the ladies and gentlemen of the jury by telling them your name and then spelling it.

A. My name is JH. JH.

Q. All right. JH, do you go by a nickname—

A. JH.

Q. What is it?

A. JH.

Q. JH, as the Court just pointed out, you are residing at the moment in DC Jail, correct?
A. Yes.
Q. And you have been convicted of multiple felonies in the past, right?
A. Yes.
Q. And you served time in prison, correct?
A. Yes.
Q. Now, in connection with any of those matters, have I or any member of the Government, any member of the police department, or any member of my office in the United States Attorney's Office offered you any deal in connection with your testimony in this case this afternoon?
A. No, sir.
Q. Now, JH, how old are you, sir?
A. Thirty-four.
Q. Before you were incarcerated, did you have a fixed address?
A. No, sir.
Q. Where did you commonly stay?
A. Over at my aunt's house, HP.
Q. Okay. And where was that?
A. 1362.
Q. What street?
A. Valley Place Southeast.
Q. All right. Do you know a person known to you as MB?
A. Yes.
Q. Who is MB?
A. She's a good friend of mine. She had a baby by one of my cousins named FG, a little son named MB.
Q. Okay. Back in April of this year, where did MB live?
A. I think it was—I can't really remember the address. 1430.
Q. What street?
A. Good Hope Road.
Q. Do you know MB's real name?
A. MB.
Q. What was right next door to MB's house?

A. My brother's barbershop.
Q. Okay. What's the name of it?
A. Cutting Up.
Q. And what's your brother's name?
A. MS.
Q. Did you ever work inside your brother's place?
A. Yes.
Q. What would you do there?
A. Mostly janitor, cleanup.
Q. Does your brother own any dogs?
A. Yes. He owns two Presa Canarios.
Q. Can you describe the size of these dogs?
A. Adam, he weighs like 175 pounds, and Eve, she weighs 165 pounds.
Q. Can you describe to us your relationship with Adam and Eve?
A. I love them, they're my dogs.
Q. What did they think about you?
A. They love me.
Q. Would you care for the dogs?
A. Yeah, I cared for the dogs. I took care of them.
Q. Would you walk the dogs?
A. Yes.
Q. Feed the dogs?
A. Yes.
Q. Let's talk about April 27 of this year, JH. Do you remember that day?
A. Yes.
Q. Where did you spend the night?
A. Over—
Q. The day before the 27th?
A. At MB's house.
Q. What part of the house did you stay in?
A. I stayed upstairs—not upstairs, like on the first floor. I slept in the living room on the floor.
Q. Okay. Did you have permission from MB to stay there?
A. Yes.

Q. So she knew you were there, correct?
A. Yes.
Q. Now, at some point that day, did you get involved with the dogs that were next door at Cutting Up?
A. Yes.
Q. Tell us about that.
A. I was walking the dogs.
Q. Well, before you started walking the dogs, why did you walk them?
A. Because they don't get out much.
Q. Okay. What time was it when you first approached the dogs to walk them?
A. Like about—I think it was like about 3:00 or 4:00 in the morning.
Q. What woke you up?
A. JB woke me up.
Q. Who is JB?
A. MB's son.
Q. Why did he wake you up?
A. He told me Adam got out of the yard. He jumped the fence.
Q. Okay. And as a result of hearing that information, what did you do?
A. I went to retrieve the dogs.
Q. Even though it was 3:00 in the morning?
A. Yes.
Q. Okay. Where was your brother?
A. He was at home with his family.
Q. Okay. So you got up; you went out. What did you do outside?
A. I got Adam, then I got Eve, and I walked the dogs.
Q. Why did you walk the dogs?
A. Because they were going to keep coming out of the yard till I walked them.
Q. Okay. Where did you walk the dogs?
A. I walked them around by the firehouse, and I always take them around my cousin's house.
Q. And where is that?
A. 1362.

Q. Okay. Any reason why you would take the dogs over there?
A. I just take them around there. That's the natural walk I do with them.
Q. Fair enough. How did you walk the dogs? In other words, how did you hold Adam, and how did you hold Eve, if you did?
A. I keep Eve on a leash because she tries to—I keep Adam—he's on call. He's not going to mess with anybody. But that particular night—
Q. What do you mean by "he's on call"?
A. He's not going to hurt anybody unless you tell him to do something.
Q. Okay. So does that mean you let him walk free?
A. Yeah.
Q. Okay. Go ahead.
A. I'm walking them, and as I was walking, I bent the corner, and my grandmother's dog was on the porch.
Q. What street are we talking about now?
A. Valley Place.
Q. Okay. Go ahead.
A. The dog was on the porch.
Q. What dog is that?
A. My grandmother's dog, GG.
Q. Okay. What kind of dog is it?
A. She's like a poodle.
Q. Okay. What's the dog's name?
A. I call her GG.
Q. GG?
A. Yeah.
Q. Okay. Go ahead.
A. Then she jumped up and started barking, and Eve got loose and ran into the yard and attacked her.
Q. Okay. Did you see Eve attack GG?
A. Yeah.
Q. And how bad was it, JH?
A. It wasn't—I mean, I pulled her—pried her off GG. I mean, she was bleeding, but she was still living. I don't think she was hurt that bad because she's living right now today.

Q. Did you—well, how close to the house did you get when you pried the dogs apart?
A. On the front porch.
Q. When you pried the dogs apart, did you notice anybody inside the house?
A. Yeah, my cousin NW.
Q. Okay. And what did you notice about your cousin NW?
A. He was in the house with one of HP's girls.
Q. Okay. And did you see NW looking at you at all?
A. Yeah. He came down the steps and opened the door like, "JH, man, what are you doing, man?" I said, "Man, Eve just attacked GG." So he was like, "Man, JH, man, shhh."
And he left the door open and went upstairs. So I yelled up there, "That's another strike against me, huh?"
Q. Okay. What else, if anything, did NW do?
MM: Objection, Your Honor. May we approach?
The Court: Uh-huh.
(Bench conference.)
MM: It's my understanding, Your Honor, that this witness would testify that NW pulled out a handgun with a laser sight and pointed the laser sight at the witness. I believe that's what he's getting ready to testify to, which I would suggest to the Court is not relevant. To the extent it's relevant, it's outweighed by unfair prejudice.
The Court: Is NW alleged to be the second assailant?
GP: Yes. That's exactly right.
The Court: Is that what this witness will testify to?
GP: Yes, sir.
MM: I don't think anyone has testified that NW was in the house.
GP: He will.
The Court: That's what I just asked him. So with that proffer, I'll allow it. Thank you.
(Open court.)
Direct examination by GP (continued):
Q. JH, did NW do anything else?
A. Yeah. He came back downstairs.

Q. And what did he do?
A. He pulled a gun out on me.
Q. And what did he do with that gun?
A. It had a laser on it, and he pointed it at my chest. He's like, "Man, JH. Man, see, man."
And I was like, "Man, goddamn, that's for me and you, cuz? That's how we're going?"
Q. What happened after that, JH?
A. He left the door open and went back upstairs with HP's girl, another girl.
Q. Did you see HP while you were there?
A. No, he wasn't home. I wish he was home.
Q. Okay. What did you do next?
A. I sat on the porch for a while, and I left the porch—I sat on the porch for a while. Then I called HP—I called NW and told him to come and get GG off the porch because he left her out there on the porch. So he came back downstairs, opened the gate, and let her in, so I left.
Q. Where did you go?
A. I went and put the dogs up at Cutting Up barbershop.
Q. Okay. And what did you do next?
A. I went back over to MB's house and went to sleep.
Q. Okay. Did there come a time when you saw HP a little later that day?
A. Probably about 9:00 that morning.
Q. All right. Tell us about that, JH.
A. Well, he came over with his father.
Q. What's his father's name?
A. DH.
Q. And how did you know that DH called?
A. Because I already knew— I knew there was going to be some bull-shit behind this dog. I just knew it. I felt it.
Q. All right. So how did you know that they were at the house?
A. I was looking out the window.
Q. Which window?
A. The window on the second floor.

Q. What did you see when you were looking out the window?
A. I saw—first I saw HP pull up. Then I saw his father pull up on the other side of the street.
Q. And then what did you see?
A. I saw HP—I saw his father get out of the van. I saw HP's mother get out of the van, my aunt, and I saw HP get out of the truck.
Q. What kind of truck was it?
A. Black truck.
Q. Anything unusual about the wheels on his truck?
A. It had spinners on it.
Q. What happened next, JH?
A. I ran into the other room and told MB, "Man, look, man, there's going to be some bullshit."
I said, "Man, tell them I ain't in here, man."
Q. What did MB do?
A. She said, "JH, man, I don't want no problems in my house. I got kids in here."
Q. Okay. What happened next?
A. So I said, "Man, it ain't like he's going to kill me." Because she said—I told her, "Man, go downstairs and tell them I'm not here."
So she went down there and told them I wasn't in there. Then she came back upstairs with her eyes all big like she just smoked some rocks or something.
Q. Okay. Was she mad at you?
A. No. She wasn't mad, but she looked terrified.
Q. What did you tell her?
A. I said, "What's the matter?" She said, "Man—"
MM: Objection to hearsay, Your Honor.
Direct examination by GP (continued):
Q. What did you tell her?
A. I said, "Man, what is the matter?" She said, "Man—"
MM: Objection.
GP: Not what she said, only what you told MB.
The Witness: Only what I told MB?
Direct examination by GP (continued):

Q. She asked you a question?
A. When she came back upstairs?
Q. Correct?
A. Yeah.
Q. Tell us what you said in response to MB's question.
A. In response to her question?
Q. Right. What did you say?
A. Like, when HP came with a gun.
Q. No. No. MB came to you and asked you a question about what had just happened, right?
A. Yeah.
Q. And you told her something, right?
A. I told her, "Well, he ain't going to kill me."
Q. Did you say anything else?
A. No.
Q. Okay. So what did you do after that—after that conversation with MB?
A. I stayed in the house, and later on that day, we had a beer or two.
Q. Who is "we"?
A. Me, MB, and SB.
Q. Okay. What happened next?
A. Around about 1:00 that day, I saw HP pull up in the truck.
Q. And how did you know—how did you happen to know it was HP pulling up in the truck?
A. Because he had a big ol' truck with spinners on it.
Q. And where were you looking from?
A. Out the top—I was in the attic. I was at the top window from the attic looking out.
Q. Okay. Go ahead. What else did you see?
A. I saw NW pull up in a silver—like a little Honda or something, like a little silver—looked like a girl's car or something.
Q. Okay. Is this the same NW that pointed the laser at you?
A. Yeah.
Q. Go ahead. What happened next?
A. NW got out of his car, and another girl, who was in the car with them, got out on the driver's side and moved the car up the

street. So I ran downstairs, and I saw this other little girl named JC. She was at the door. I told her, "Don't open the door."
Q. On the inside or the outside?
A. On the inside of the house.
Q. Okay. What did you tell—
A. I told her, "Man, don't open this door, man." She said, "Why? Why?" I said, "Man, because it's going to be some bullshit if you open this door."
So she looked out the window, saw the big ol' truck, and saw the spinners still spinning. It wouldn't stop. She's like, "Ooh, ooh, I'm letting them in. I'm letting them in."
I said, "Man, don't open that door." So she turned the knob and opened the door. So I took the door and pushed it back with my foot.
Q. And—go ahead. With your foot?
A. Yeah. I slammed it back with my foot. So he's going to tell me—he said, "JH, man, you're going to get away from this door. Don't make me start shooting through this door."
Q. Who said that?
A. HP.
Q. All right. Go ahead.
A. So I hauled ass upstairs to the attic.
Q. What happened once you got to the attic?
A. I just heard somebody keep calling my name, "JH, JH, JH."
Q. Did you recognize the voice?
A. Yeah.
Q. Who was it?
A. HP.
Q. All right. What happened then?
A. He's like, "JH, JH. Where you at, JH?" I guess he was looking through the house, trying to see where I was at.
Q. So that voice was coming from the outside now or inside the house?
A. Inside the house. He was already inside the house.
Q. All right. What happened next, JH?

A. Someway, he found his way up into the attic. And I was like, "HP, HP, let me talk to you. Let me talk to you."

He just started crying. He said, "JH, man, JH, man, that's Grandma's dog, that's Grandma's dog."

The Court: You've got to slow down just a little, sir.

The Witness: He's like, "JH, man, JH, man, that's Grandma's dog." My grandmother died in a fire, and they saved the dog from the fire, so I could see how emotional he was about it. That's how I knew there was going to be some bullshit behind the dog.

Q. And what happened after that?

A. After that, he raised his gun and was like pow (*indicating*). He said, "JH, man." I said, "HP, HP, HP, it's not for me, you know. It's not for me." I said, "Ask NW. Ask NW. I didn't sic these dogs on Grandma Grady."

Q. Where was NW?

A. He was standing on the attic steps.

Q. Where was HP? Was he on the steps or up in the attic?

A. He was up in the attic, facing me.

Q. Okay. Was he near the steps?

A. No. He wasn't near the steps. He was backed up some.

Q. All right. And where did he point the gun when he—

A. He pointed it at me.

Q. Okay. How many times did he shoot?

A. He shot four times in the attic, and when he was about to leave, he shot two more shots going up, coming up in the attic.

Q. All right. Tell us about that. He confronted you—HP confronted you in the attic, correct?

A. Yeah.

Q. All right. Tell us again what he said as he confronted you.

A. He said, "JH, man—"

MM: Objection. Asked and answered.

The Court: Overruled.

The Witness: "JH, man, that's Grandma's dog." I said, "HP, HP, let me talk to you, man." I said, "Ask NW. Ask NW." He said—NW was looking at me all dumbfounded. I said, "NW, tell him, man. Tell him."

Pow. I said, "HP, HP, come on." *Pow.* I just heard a bullet whistle past my ear. *Boom.* I said, "HP, HP." That's when I took cover behind the wall.

So he fired again, *pow.* I said, "Oh, shit."

Then NW was like—I said—then I said, "Man, MB is going to call the police."

So HP didn't say anything. NW did like this, waving him, telling him to come on. So they left. As HP was leaving down the steps, he fired two more shots.

Q. Did he ever hit you with a bullet?

A. No. A bullet never hit me.

Q. Okay. What happened after they left your sight?

A. I jumped over—I went downstairs to the second floor and walked into MB's room to see if anyone was in there. When I looked in, I guess MB heard my footsteps, and he pulled the cover back and looked at me. He said, "JH, you okay? You all right?" We were so scared. I wanted to cry because I was thinking, "Goddamn, I shouldn't have brought this into his mother's house like this, but I didn't know it was going to go that far."

Q. So what did you do next?

A. I climbed off the back balcony in his mother's room and jumped over my brother's fence.

Q. Into the barbershop property?

A. Yes.

Q. What did you do over there?

A. I let the dogs out in the yard, let them play around a little bit, and then headed out.

Q. All right. Now, did there come a time, JH, when you placed a 911 call?

A. I placed two of them.

Q. Two of them, okay. When did you make those calls?

A. The same day, right after the incident.

Q. Okay. I'd like to play those calls for you. You can listen, and then I'll ask you a couple of questions afterward, okay?

A. All right.

(First call. Audio being played, not reported.)

(Second call. Audio being played, not reported.)

DIRECT EXAMINATION BY GP (CONTINUED):

Q. JH, did you make those two 911 calls that we just heard?
A. Yes.
Q. Now, it's clear from both calls that you did not want to be identified as JH, correct?
A. Yeah.
Q. Why is that?
A. 'Cause I just—I don't know. I was just scared.
Q. Scared of what?
A. About the whole incident. I didn't know whether I was shot or not. I was just mad because he's family. Why would you do something like this? You know what I mean?
Q. All right. And you also provided a false name, didn't you?
A. Yeah.
Q. What name did you give?
A. Elvis.
Q. Spell that.
A. I don't even know how to spell it. I ain't going to lie to you.
Q. And why did you do that?
A. Because I didn't want to be interviewed. I didn't want to bring a whole lot of heat to MB's house about me being down there like that.
Q. So aside from the false name and the fact that you didn't identify who you were, was everything else that we heard true?
A. Yeah.
Q. At some point, did the police arrive at MB's house?
A. Yeah.
Q. Where were you when they started arriving?
A. I was still over the gate, hiding in my brother's backyard.
Q. Did there ever come a time when you talked to the police?
A. Yeah, I talked to one female police officer.
Q. How did they find you?
A. Because Eve was back there throwing a bowl up in the air. She had a big iron bowl, and she was just throwing it up in the air and making noise. So the female officer came back there, peeked

behind the little covers on the fence, and she saw me. She said, "Oh, there you go right there, JH." She said, "Why was your cousin shooting at you?" I said, "My cousin wasn't shooting at me."

Q. Why did you say that?

A. I don't know why. I didn't want to get him in trouble.

Q. Why didn't you come out immediately when the police started arriving at the house?

A. I don't know. I'm already bipolar and schizophrenic. I just don't know why.

Q. Now—

A. I just felt safer back there with the dogs.

Q. Now, when you did talk to the police, there came a time when they asked you about the events, correct?

A. Yeah.

Q. And who did you tell them was responsible for coming into the house and shooting?

A. I didn't tell them anybody.

Q. Initially, correct?

A. I didn't tell them anybody initially. I never even talked to detectives or anything. After they found out I had a warrant out on me, they put me in a holding cell and took me down to central cellblock ASAP.

Q. But at some point, you came to my office, didn't you?

A. Yeah.

Q. And there was a detective with us, correct?

A. Detective Francis. That's right. Timothy Francis.

Q. And at that point, you provided Detective Francis and myself with further information, correct?

A. Yes.

Q. What did you tell us, or who did you tell us was responsible?

A. HP.

Q. Was that the truth?

A. Yes.

Q. Now, during that same meeting, out of my presence, you were shown a photograph, correct?

A. Yeah.
Q. You remember that?
A. Yeah.
Q. And who was that a photograph of?
A. HP.
Q. All right. JH, I'm showing you Government's Exhibit Number 13. Take a look at that. Have you seen that photograph before?
A. Yes.
Q. What is it?
A. That's HP right there.
Q. Is that the same photograph that you were presented by Detective Francis?
A. Yes.
Q. And did Detective Francis ask you questions in connection with showing you that photograph?
A. Yes.
Q. And did you respond to those questions?
A. Yes.
Q. What did you tell Detective Francis while you were looking at that photograph?
A. I told him that's my cousin right there.
Q. And what did you say about your cousin's responsibility for what happened at the house on Good Hope Road?
A. What did I say about his responsibility?
Q. Right. What did you tell Detective Francis that your cousin had done?
MM: I do object to the witness reading the notes.
GP: I'll take it away.
Direct examination by GP (continued):
Q. What did you tell Detective Francis that your cousin HP had done?
A. He shot at me.
Q. Shot at you?
A. Yeah.
Q. At 1435 Good Hope Road?
A. Yes.

GP: At this time, I move for the admission of Government's Exhibit Number 13, Your Honor.
THE COURT: Admitted.
(Government's Exhibit Number 13 admitted into evidence.)
DIRECT EXAMINATION BY GP (CONTINUED):
Q. JH, what relationship do you have with HP?
A. He's my cousin.
Q. How so?
A. Through my uncle—my uncle DH, my father's brother.
Q. So your father and HP's father are brothers?
A. Yes.
Q. And did you have anything against HP before this dog incident arose?
A. No. We were cool.
Q. In fact, you lived in the same house, didn't you?
A. Yeah.
Q. Do you see your cousin—your first cousin HP—in the courtroom today?
A. He's right there.
Q. What color shirt is he wearing?
A. Yellow shirt.
GP: Your Honor, may the record reflect that the witness has provided an in-court identification of HP.
THE COURT: The record will so reflect.
GP: Court's indulgence.
DIRECT EXAMINATION BY GP (CONTINUED):
Q. Now, JH, you received a visit a couple of nights ago from Attorney MM, didn't you?
A. Yes, sir.
Q. Did you talk to Attorney MM?
A. I talked to him on numerous occasions.
Q. Okay. And what story did you tell MM about what happened at 1435 Good Hope Road?
A. I told him—
MM: Objection, Your Honor, to hearsay.
THE COURT: Sustained at this point.

Direct examination by GP (continued):

Q. Did you tell MM the truth about what happened?

A. I told him the truth about five times. He came to see me like five times. I told him the truth, then I got a message from other inmates when I was over at CTF.

MM: Objection, Your Honor.

The Court: Sustained.

Direct examination by GP (continued):

Q. Did you ever—did you ever tell MM—

MM: May we approach, Your Honor?

The Court: Um-hmm.

(Bench conference.)

MM: Truth be told, I'm going to be asking this witness a lot of the same questions.

GP: And I—

The Court: Well, that's fine, but technically it's his choice to put it in. So—

GP: Very well.

The Court: Now—

MM: So I object.

The Court: Yeah. So technically, you have to wait. Thank you.

(Open court.)

Direct examination by GP (continued):

Q. The version that you told today, JH, is it truthful?

A. Yes.

GP: I have no further questions. Thank you.

Cross-examination by MM:

Q. Hello, JH.

A. Hello.

Q. JH, you were talking about—what GP was asking you about—talking to me. Is that right? You talked to me a number of times. Is that right?

A. Yeah. I talked to you numerous times.

Q. Okay. Thank you.

A. Most recently, like two nights ago?

Q. Yeah. You and I had a chat at the jail, correct?

A. Yeah.
Q. Okay. And, in fact, during one of those conversations, you gave me a written statement, didn't you?
A. Yeah, awhile back.
Q. A couple—it was a couple—two months ago or something like that?
A. Yeah.
Q. Back in—more than that—it was back in July, wasn't it?
A. I think it was.
Q. Okay. And what you ended up telling me and my investigator, Dale Vaughn—do you remember him?
A. I think I do.
Q. Do you remember meeting with me and another middle-aged white guy?
A. I remember meeting you. I really don't remember his face or what I talked to him about, but I know what I talked to you about.
Q. Okay. And one of the things you told me was that on April 27, when all this happened, you were actually in the basement, right?
A. Yeah, at that particular time. What I told you prior to that—all the other times I told you—I told you the same thing. I'm telling you what I told GP happened.
Q. All right. So we're going to take them one at a time, if you don't mind. Would that be okay with you, JH?
A. Yeah.
Q. All right. The meeting that I'm talking about in July—you told me you were down in the basement, and you heard some shots upstairs. Isn't that right?
A. Yeah, I told you that.
Q. All right. You also told me that you waited and then came upstairs. Isn't that right?
A. Yes, I told you that.
Q. All right. You told me there were a bunch of people out on the sidewalk. Isn't that right?
A. Yes, sir. I told you.
Q. You also told me that you never saw the shooter. Isn't that right?

A. Yes, I told you that.
Q. Okay. And then you told me you went out the back, then went to hide because you were worried that you had a warrant. Isn't that right?
A. Yes, I told you that.
Q. All right. And as it turns out, you did have a warrant, isn't that right?
A. Yes.
Q. And as a matter of fact, as GP asked you, you have some prior convictions, correct?
A. Yeah.
Q. And, in fact, you have a pending case right now for assault with a dangerous weapon, correct?
A. Yes, I do.
Q. And you're being prosecuted by the US Attorney's Office for that case, correct?
A. Yes, I am.
Q. And the Government just made a plea offer to you in that case, isn't that right? Just yesterday, isn't that right?
A. What plea offer?
Q. Well, I'm asking you. Have they made a plea offer in your case—
A. The prosecutor offered me three years.
Q. Um-hmm.
A. And to tell on the guy who stabbed me.
Q. Okay. As a matter of fact, one of the conditions of the plea offer they made to you was that you agree to provide truthful and complete information to the US Attorney's Office about any matter for which they request, correct?
A. I didn't understand that part.
Q. Well, you're charged with assault with a dangerous weapon, correct?
A. Yes.
Q. In that case?
A. Yes.
Q. And you're aware the maximum penalty for that is ten years, correct?

A. I guess.
Q. And they made you a plea offer of attempted assault with a dangerous weapon. Is that right?
A. Yeah. But I didn't take the plea offer. I don't want that plea offer.
Q. But you do hope that they make you a good plea offer, correct?
A. I hope they just let me go because I'm innocent.
Q. But you don't want to do any more time in jail, correct?
A. I'm a victim.
Q. I'm not saying you're not. I'm asking you if you want to do more time in jail?
A. I mean, if I have to—I did fifteen years already. So if I have to, it won't be a problem, but I'm the victim right now.
Q. So you want to do more time in jail?
A. No, I don't want to do more time.
Q. I see.
A. But if I have to, then I will. I know how to do time. That's what I'm trying to tell you.
Q. Now, during that meeting on July 14, 2011, you also told me that the only reasonable—strike that. Let me ask you another question. You were saying that at some other meetings with me, you told me the same story that you just testified to today. Isn't that right?
A. Yes. Didn't I tell you those stories, too? The same stories?
Q. Well, actually, you're not allowed to ask questions.
A. Oh.
Q. But you did tell me that same story, right?
A. Yes, millions of times.
Q. More than once, right?
A. Yeah.
Q. And you told that to GP, isn't that right?
A. Yes.
Q. More than once?
A. Yes.
Q. But in that meeting on July 14, 2011, you told me that you signed a statement saying that the only reason you said those things is because that's what MB told you to say?

A. Yeah. But I did that because I got—
Q. Let me ask you—
A. —from an inmate.
GP: Objection.
Cross-examination by MM (continued):
Q. Why you did it—
A. I got word from another inmate telling me—
The Court: Okay. One second, sir. Sir, we're not going to open any doors here. Can you come to the bench?
MM: Yes, sir.
(Bench conference.)
The Court: I just want to make sure we're not—
GP: I think the door is already opened, Your Honor.
The Court: Well, hold on one second. That's what I'm trying to ask MM, whether or not any doors were consciously opened.
MM: Doors are definitely not consciously opened, Your Honor. And I don't think the door is all the way open, and I'm done with this line of inquiry.
The Court: Okay. We'll move on, and I'm going to ask you to approach the bench if you want to redress—
GP: I do.
The Court: —any of these things in redirect.
GP: Yes, Your Honor.
The Court: I want to hear the rest of it.
GP: Yes, Your Honor.
(Open court.)
Cross-examination by MM (continued):
Q. JH, when the police first interviewed you—excuse me—when the police first talked to you on April 27, 2011, that was in the backyard behind MB's house, isn't that right?
A. Um-hmm.
Q. And what you told police was that you heard some shots and that you jumped out a window and didn't see who was doing the shooting. Isn't that right?
A. No, I didn't tell the police that.
Q. You didn't tell them that at all?

A. Naw.
Q. And another thing you told the police was that you thought HP was out to get you, isn't that right?
A. No, I didn't tell the police that.
Q. And another thing that you told them is that you thought HP was out to get you because you saw him shoot up the barbershop a year earlier. Isn't that right?
A. No, I didn't tell the police that.
Q. You were present when that barbershop got shot up, weren't you?
A. Yeah, I was there.
Q. It was not HP, isn't that right?
A. Naw.
Q. And you're saying you didn't tell the police officers that it was?
A. No, I never did.
Q. Was Elvis the name you gave to the police?
A. Yeah.
Q. Like Elvis Presley? Elvis like that?
A. Yeah, something like that.
Q. Your testimony is that the shooting took place in the attic, correct?
A. Yeah.
Q. You weren't in any other room in the house when the shooting was going on, right? It was just the attic, isn't that right?
A. Yeah, in the attic.
Q. And after you left the attic, you came down into the second floor, then you went into MB's room, correct?
A. Yes.
Q. And there you saw MB, correct?
A. And my cousin.
Q. I'm sorry?
A. My little cousin.
Q. Your little—nine-year-old at the time, correct?
A. Yeah.
Q. And he was under the covers, right?
A. He was scared.
Q. When you came down the steps, how soon after the shooting did you go down the steps?

A. I was going to go down behind them, but my conscience told me not to. Once I listened to my conscience, that's when I heard the two shots coming up the steps.

Q. So how much time—are you saying those two shots were HP standing on the steps shooting up into the attic?

A. He was walking down the steps, shooting up into the attic.

Q. All right. How much time went by between those two shots—

A. I don't know.

Q. —and when you got out of there?

The Court: Hold on one second. We need a question, a pause, and an answer for the court reporter. Thank you.

MM: You're right, Your Honor.

Cross-examination by MM (continued):

Q. Excuse me, JH. I'll slow down. Are you able to estimate for the Court how much time went by between the time you heard those two shots and the time you went down the attic steps?

A. Like—a couple seconds.

Q. And when you went down the steps, you did not see MB in the hallway, correct?

A. No.

Q. You didn't see MB until you went into that bedroom, right?

A. Yeah, until he pulled the cover off him. That's when I saw him.

Q. Okay. And your testimony is that you went to the door and that JC was going to open the door for HP and NW because she was infatuated with the spinners on his car, is that right?

A. Yeah.

Q. So in that room, it was you and JC, correct?

A. Me and JC.

Q. Anybody else in that room?

A. MB. I think she was in the kitchen drinking a beer, and SH.

Q. You say you think she was, or she was?

A. She was because—she was in there.

Q. Okay. So MB was not at the front door with you, correct?

A. Correct. No, she was not at the front door with me.

Q. Okay. And that door actually opened. You had to push it—you had to push it closed, correct?

A. Pushed it back shut.
Q. And then, according to you, according to your testimony, you let go of the door and you hightailed it up the stairs, correct?
A. Yeah.
Q. And that's when these two guys came in, correct?
A. Yeah.
Q. Right behind you, right?
A. I ain't—yes.
Q. Okay. And you say MB was in the kitchen drinking?
A. Um-hmm.
Q. Okay. Was she in there with anybody else?
A. With a lady named SH.
Q. And what was she drinking, MB I mean?
A. ——.
Q. And you had drunk some —— that day as well, correct?
A. Yes.
Q. In fact, you had drunk three ——, correct?
A. Yeah.
Q. They were forty-ounce ——, correct?
A. Twenty-four ounces.
Q. Twenty-four ounces, okay. And you drank three of them?
A. Yeah.
Q. And you also—you had smoked some weed, correct?
A. Not that particular day. I don't think so.
Q. Do you remember talking to me three nights ago?
A. Three nights ago?
Q. Yeah. Two nights ago, do you remember talking to me?
A. Yeah, I remember talking to you.
Q. Do you remember telling me that you had smoked some weed?
A. Yeah, but I think I told that to the—I don't know whether I smoked some that day or not, but you asked me if I smoke weed. I said I don't smoke it like that. I said I might take about three or four pulls off of it and pass it back to somebody who gave it to me. That's what I believe I told you.
Q. All right. Well, let me make it easy for you. Did you take a few pulls that day?

A. I can't remember.
Q. But you told me you did a couple of nights ago, right?
A. I probably did tell you I did.
Q. All right. When you were living at—or staying over there with MB on Good Hope Road, did you own a gun?
A. No, I don't own guns.
GP: Objection.
The Court: Overruled.
Cross-examination by MM (continued):
Q. Did you have a gun in the house?
A. I never had a gun.
Q. Was there a gun in the house?
GP: Objection.
The Witness: No.
The Court: Overruled.
Cross-examination by MM (continued):
Q. Now, there's a lot of people back at that time, you know, April 2011, that used to hang around at—at MB's house. Isn't that right?
GP: Objection.
The Witness: Yeah.
The Court: Overruled.
Cross-examination by MM (continued):
Q. They used to hang out in front of the house, correct?
A. Yeah.
Q. And a lot of those people were doing drugs out in front of the house, correct?
GP: Objection. Relevance.
The Witness: Not that I know of.
The Court: Hold on one second. Sustained, unless you can tie it up today.
MM: I'll move on, Your Honor.
Cross-examination by MM (continued):
Q. Now, after you—you came home after this dog incident—after, I guess it was Eve, was it, that had attacked Grandma Grady? Is that right?

A. Yeah.

Q. All right. After that, you went home, and you were looking for someone to come over to the house. Isn't that right?

A. I was—I knew it was going to be some bullshit behind this dog.

Q. You knew there was going to be bullshit behind the dog, right?

A. Yeah. I just knew it. I just knew it.

Q. Sorry. I'll give a pause, Your Honor. I caught myself that time.

THE COURT: Thank you.

MM: Sorry, JH.

THE COURT: It's for the court reporter. Thank you.

MM: I'm sorry, ma'am.

CROSS-EXAMINATION BY MM (CONTINUED):

Q. I mean, you were literally sitting up on the second floor looking out of your window just waiting for somebody to come over, right?

A. I was paranoid. I'm already schizophrenic.

Q. And were you taking your medication that day?

A. No. I haven't taken my medication in a while.

MM: And—may we approach, Your Honor.

THE COURT: Um-hmm.

(Bench conference.)

MM: I just wanted to alert the Court and mostly GP that I intend on asking him what kind of medication he takes and what effect it has on him and that sort of thing.

THE COURT: That's fair.

(Open court.)

CROSS-EXAMINATION BY MM (CONTINUED):

Q. JH, what type of—what type of medication, if you know, are you prescribed for paranoid schizophrenia?

A. I take—I take—I take Depakote.

Q. Depakote?

A. For depression.

Q. Okay.

A. I take—I take Risperdal. That's for my schizophrenia. And I take Elavil to help me sleep.

Q. All right. The Risperdal, do you know what your prescription was—how much you were supposed to take?
A. Three milligrams.
Q. Is that supposed to be daily?
A. Yeah, every day.
Q. And what happens to you, in your own experience, when you don't take the Risperdal?
A. I can't sleep. I have racing thoughts. I be depressed, real lonely.
Q. All right. Do you ever have, you know, hallucinations or anything along those lines?
A. Naw, I don't know.
Q. You don't know, okay. And how long had it been since you had taken your Risperdal—let me focus you. On April 27, 2011, when all this happened, how long had it been since you had taken your Risperdal?
A. I haven't taken it in a while. I can't tell you how long it's been.
Q. Was it more than a couple of months?
A. Up until that point I got locked up for this incident. When I had the warrant, and they locked me up for this whole incident, that's—when I got locked up, I started taking my medication again.
Q. All right. Well, I'm asking you about the period of time before that actually. Before you got locked up. You actually got locked up the same day that this all happened, right?
A. Yeah.
Q. Okay. So before that, how long had it been since you had taken the Risperdal?
A. I can't remember.
Q. Do you know whether it was more than a month?
A. It probably was longer than that.
Q. Now, at the scene—and by the scene, I mean on Good Hope Road—when those police officers came over—came over to talk to you, you did not tell them it was HP. Isn't that right?
A. No. I told them—I told them HP wasn't shooting at me.
Q. In fact, you told them HP wasn't shooting at you, correct?
A. That's what I told them.

Q. Um-hmm. And you never told them that you saw HP in the house. Isn't that right?
A. They didn't ask me that.
Q. All right. But you never told them that HP had come by earlier. Isn't that right?
A. No. I never told them none of that.
Q. So to recap your testimony today is that HP came into the house and shot in your direction when you were up in the attic, correct?
A. Yeah.
Q. But what you told the police that day was that that didn't happen and that HP didn't do that, correct?
A. Yes.
Q. And what you told me in July was that you were in the basement and you did hear shots, but you didn't see who was shooting, correct?
A. Yes.
MM: Thank you, sir.
GP: May we approach?
The Court: Uh-huh.
(Bench conference.)
GP: Your Honor, I believe the Government is totally entitled to inquire of JH as to the reason why he told MM a different story and reasons why he may have told the police officers a different story, but I'm primarily focused on why he talked to MM a couple nights ago.
The Court: And what is your proffer?
GP: Quite frankly, I don't know. But I think that he's entitled to explain the reasons why he told a different version of the issue.
MM: If I may interject, Your Honor. I think if GP is worried more about two nights ago; two nights ago was an occasion when JH told me a story consistent with the Government's theory of the case. The version he gave me that was inconsistent was in July. And so I mentioned that.
The Court: This is—this is where I am on this.

I interjected myself because the witness was offering answers. My reading of the latest Court of Appeals opinion on this is that unless—well, the inference that I was taking from the witness is that somebody at the jail told him something that scared him off. My reading of the Court of Appeals decision most recently has been that unless there's evidence tying those actions or those influences to the defendant, the Court of Appeals has instructed us the evidence is so prejudicial that the Court should rarely introduce it. So that's what I'm concerned about. And that's where I thought the witness was going, which is why I interjected myself.

GP: I understand the Court's position. However, I still believe that the Government should be entitled with obvious limitation to permit this witness to rehabilitate himself as to—

The Court: I have—I have no problem with that, consistent with the Court of Appeals instructions that I'm supposed to protect the improper inference unless there's evidence that the defendant—so if you're proposing to lead the witness in a fashion that doesn't make it look like he—that it was influences by the defendant, I'll hear you on that. But that's what I'm concerned about.

GP: May I propose a question?

The Court: (*Nods.*) I'll hear your proposal on the type of question.

GP: I would simply ask JH if—first of all—if the answer that he provided MM back in July was truthful. The presumption is that he would say no. What is the reason for—

The Court: That's what the Court of Appeals told us not to do.

GP: "Is the reason for the falsehood based upon your recollection of actual events or some other reason?"

The Court: Make sure he doesn't answer "the other reason."

MM: I don't know how GP is going to make sure that he doesn't do that.

The Court: That's a very dangerous—

MM: I would ask through the Court if GP knows what this communication at the jail was.

GP: I have no idea.

MM: I think that's part of the problem.

GP: Should—should—should we excuse the jury, Your Honor?

The Court: No. This is what I'm proposing you say. You—I'll give you multiple questions for emphasis as a trade-off about whether or not the statement he told MM in July was true. Did he know it was true at the time, and is what he told the jury and what he told you true?

GP: All right. May I also—may I ask him about his grand jury testimony for prior consistent statements?

The Court: Yeah. I think that's true. Do you have a problem with that?

MM: I do, but I don't have a good objection.

Redirect examination by GP:

Q. Why did he not want you to open the door? Explain to the ladies and gentlemen what happened next.

A. Um, it was a knock at the door. Um, it was JH's uncle, and he asked if JH was in the house.

Q. Now, how did you know it was JH's uncle?

A. JH—evidently JH saw them and told me to go to the door and say he wasn't in the house.

Q. Okay. Go ahead. What happened then?

A. I go downstairs, and I answer my door. The young man said—

MM: Objection to the hearsay, Your Honor.

The Court: Overruled.

Redirect examination by GP (continued):

Q. What did he say?

A. He asked if JH was in the house.

Q. Now, was this HP or the other man?

A. It was the other guy.

Q. Okay. And had you opened the door to talk to him?

A. Yes.

Q. Okay. Go ahead.

A. I—I opened the door. I said, "JH is not in here." And he said, "Do you know where he's at?" I said, "No." And, um, my two sons, they were looking out my side window.

Q. Which two sons?

A. AB and MB.
Q. Go ahead.
The Court: Okay. Great. Thank you.
(Open court.)
Redirect examination by GP (continued):
Q. JH, hello again.
A. Hey.
The Court: JH, I'm just going to ask you to listen to GP's questions and only answer the questions that are proposed to you.
The Witness: Okay.
The Court: Okay.
Redirect examination by GP (continued):
Q. JH, you—you testified—this isn't the first time you testified in connection with this case, correct?
A. Right.
Q. And, in fact, you testified in front of the grand jury back in May of this year, correct?
A. Yeah.
Q. Do you remember that?
A. Yes.
Q. And, in fact, that was the same day that you and I met and the same day that you met Detective Timothy Francis. Do you remember that?
A. Yeah.
Q. And I was the assistant United States attorney that was in the grand jury with you asking you questions, correct?
A. Yes.
Q. And you were sworn to tell the truth that day, weren't you?
A. Yeah.
MM: I need page and line.
GP: Just to solidify your recollection, JH, you see the date here was May—and I'm showing you Government's Number 45, which is a transcript of your grand jury testimony. Do you see the date, Tuesday, May 31?
A. Um-hmm.
Q. Do you see your name there?

A. Yeah.

Q. Okay. Now, on that date, did you not provide testimony consistent with what you testified to today, sir?

A. Yes.

Q. Counsel, page 25, lines 14 and 21. Do you remember me asking you these questions and you providing these answers, JH?

Question: "Okay. What happened?"

Answer: "So she tried to open the door. I pushed the door back, so somebody pushed the door. Boom, boom. I said, 'Man, what the fuck?' So he said, 'Man, JH, you don't open this door, I'm going to shoot through the fucking door. Open the door.'"

Question: "Who said that?"

Answer: "HP."

The Witness: HP.

Q. Do you remember making that statement?

A. Yes.

Q. Was it truthful then?

A. Yes, that's true.

Q. That's what you said today, right?

A. Yeah.

Q. Counsel, page 27, lines 12 through 17.

Question: "Okay. Go ahead."

Your answer: "So he said, 'JH man, why you do that?' I said, 'Man, hold up. Let me talk to you. I didn't—indecipherable—the dog on Grandma's dog.' I said, 'The dog should have been in the house. You know, Uncle David said keep the dog in the house.' He said, 'Man JH,' *pow*. He fired one shot at me. I was like, yeah. So I stopped, and I looked at him."

Do you remember that?

A. Um-hmm.

Q. Is that statement true?

A. Yes.

Q. That's consistent with how you testified today, correct?

A. Yeah.

Q. Counsel, page 28, lines 18 and 19.

Question: "Did he aim the gun at you?"

Answer: "Yes."

You were asked, JH, about a conversation you had with MM back in July.

A. Um-hmm.

Q. And when you had that conversation with MM, you told him a different version than what you told the grand jury back in May and what you told this jury today in October, correct?

A. Um-hmm.

Q. Is that correct?

A. Yeah.

Q. Now, which version—I'll ask you this one time—which version is correct and the truth?

A. This version.

Q. The grand jury version?

A. Yep.

Q. And what about your trial testimony today?

A. The truth.

Q. You were—you were offered a cooperation agreement?

GP: Your Honor, we'll mark this as Government's 44.

Redirect examination by GP (continued):

Q. Approaching you, JH, with Government's Exhibit Number 44. Have you seen this cooperation agreement? Have you read it?

A. I never even read this. He presented it to me, he read some stuff to me, and I told him I ain't want it.

Q. Okay. In fact, there's a space there—there's a line for signature, isn't it?

A. Yeah.

Q. It's under defendant's acknowledgment. Do you see your signature there?

A. No.

Q. Why is that?

A. Because I'm innocent.

Q. But why—why isn't your signature on this document?

A. Because I haven't signed it.

Q. So in short, has the Government offered you anything in connection with this case?

A. No.
Q. The case in which you're being held in the DC Jail now?
A. No.
Q. And you don't expect to get anything from the Government, do you?
A. No.
Q. In fact, you intend to fight these charges, don't you?
A. Yeah.
Q. Were you drunk that day?
A. What day?
Q. April 27?
A. April 27, when the incident happened?
Q. That's right.
A. I was tipsy.
Q. Were you intoxicated?
A. No, I wasn't intoxicated.
Q. Were you—were you unable to appreciate the events that were taking place?
A. I wasn't—I wasn't intoxicated. I wasn't—I was tipsy. I wasn't drunk.
Q. Now, you were honest enough to mention the mental issues that—that you wrestle with?
A. Yeah.
Q. As of April 27, did those deficiencies, if you will, cause you to imagine the events that took place inside 1435 Good Hope Road?
A. Naw.
Q. Did they cause you to hallucinate those events?
A. No.
Q. Did they cause you to misrecollect those events in any way?
MM: Objection to leading at this stage.
The Court: Overruled. He's just tying it up.
Redirect examination by GP (continued):
Q. Why did you tell—why—a better question is, why did you not tell the responding police officers who the shooter was?
A. Because MB's kids was there, and I didn't want to bring a lot attention to her house because she didn't want no more prob-

lems in her house. I just—I think I probably was scared. I don't know. I'm already schizophrenic. I just wanted to hide out and just be safe.

Q. And, lastly, why didn't you mention to the police officers the earlier—the morning encounter or the morning visit by HP?

A. Because I haven't—I ain't seen no gun. She just came back upstairs and told me he had a gun.

Q. So why didn't you tell the police that he was even there?

A. Why haven't I told the police he was there?

Q. Why did you not tell the police when they came to the house that he had been there earlier?

A. I don't know.

Q. But is that to suggest that it didn't happen?

A. It did happen.

GP: I have nothing further, Your Honor.

THE COURT: Thank you.

Ladies and gentlemen, we'll take a short recess now and get set up for the next witness. Do not discuss the case among yourselves or with anyone else during the course of the recess. Thank you very much. You can go. Just leave your pads in the seat.

(Jury out.)

THE COURT: Thank you, JH. Thank you, Marshal.

(Witness excused.)

(Brief recess.)

(Jury in.)

THE COURT: Next witness.

GP: Government calls Officer Walter Smith.

(Thereupon, WALTER SMITH, having been called as a witness on behalf of the Government and having been first duly sworn by the deputy clerk, was examined and testified.)

DIRECT EXAMINATION BY GP (CONTINUED):

Q. Officer Smith, good afternoon, sir.

A. Good afternoon.

Q. How you doing, sir?

A. Good.

Q. Officer, introduce yourself to the ladies and gentlemen of the jury by telling them what your name is and then spelling it.
A. My name is Officer Smith, S-m-i-t-h. First name is Walter.
The Court: Ladies and gentlemen, Officer Smith was not introduced by name to you at—during jury selection, so this is the first time we're mentioning his name. Does anybody in the jury know Officer Smith? No affirmative response. Thank you. GP.
Direct examination by GP (continued):
Q. Officer Smith, you're employed by the Metropolitan Police Department, correct?
A. Yes, sir.
Q. How long have you worked there?
A. Just over three years.
Q. And what's your current rank and duty assignment?
A. I'm an officer assigned to patrol, day shift.
Q. In what area of the city are you assigned? 7-D, southeast?
A. Yes, sir.
Q. Does the Seventh District encompass the 1400-block of Good Hope Road, Southeast?
A. Yes, sir.
Q. And is that Washington, DC?
A. Yes, sir.
Q. Did you have an opportunity, Officer Smith, to respond to a home located at 1435 Good Hope Road, Southeast, on the afternoon of April 27 of this year?
A. Yes, sir.
Q. Were you working alone, or did you have a partner that day?
A. I had a partner.
Q. And what was your partner's name?
A. Officer Pulaski.
Q. First name?
A. Chelsea.
Q. What was the reason for your response to that location with Officer Pulaski?
A. We had a radio call for a burglary B-1 in progress that was attached to a shooting.

Q. When you got the call, do you recall how long it took you to respond to the 1400-block?
A. No, sir.
Q. When you got there, what did you observe?
A. Myself and Officer Pulaski, we got there. I pulled up probably about a half—half a house off. As soon as I got there, the witness inside the house, the homeowner, came outside.
Q. Do you remember who that was?
A. Not by name, no.
Q. Male or female?
A. Female.
Q. All right. Go ahead.
A. She came outside. My partner went on and started speaking to her. I actually went to the back of the—of the house just to secure it just in case the individuals were still inside.
Q. Were you and your partner the first officers to respond to the scene?
A. Yes, sir.
Q. What, if anything, happened after that?
A. My partner came out. She explained to me what happened and gave me a lookout of a vehicle that was possibly involved with the burglary and shooting.
Q. What was that lookout?
A. It was supposed to be for a black SUV with chrome spinning rims.
Q. Were you familiar with that vehicle?
A. Yes, sir.
Q. And were you familiar with the individual that either owned or drove that vehicle?
A. Yes, sir.
Q. When was the last time you had seen that vehicle that was described to you in the lookout?
MM: Objection, Your Honor. May we approach?
The Court: Um-hmmm.
The Witness: Step down?
The Court: Thank you.
(Bench conference.)

THE COURT: Um-hmmm.

MM: I have an objection to the characterization of the question "that vehicle." I have no objection to ask him if he saw a similar vehicle at any other time, but he's making—

GP: It was a terrible question.

THE COURT: Thank you.

(Open court.)

DIRECT EXAMINATION BY GP (CONTINUED):

Q. Officer Smith, who was the individual that you associated with the lookout vehicle?

A. The person that was associated with the vehicle would have been HP.

Q. Do you see Mr. HP in the courtroom today?

A. Yes, sir.

Q. Please point him out and describe the color of his shirt.

A. He is sitting to my left with the yellow shirt on, with the glasses.

THE COURT: May the record reflect that the officer has provided an in-court identification of HP. Record will so reflect.

DIRECT EXAMINATION BY GP (CONTINUED):

Q. How long had you known HP?

A. Nine months, maybe a year.

Q. Based upon the description that you received of the vehicle in the lookout, did it occur to you that you had seen that vehicle earlier?

A. Earlier in the day, yes, sir.

Q. And where did you see the vehicle?

A. I first saw it early that morning in front of 1362 Valley Place.

Q. And did you see HP in the proximity of that vehicle?

A. Yes, sir.

Q. And where exactly did you see HP?

A. He was around the passenger side of that vehicle.

Q. Going back to the 1400-block of Good Hope Road, what, if anything, happened after you received the information about that vehicle from your car?

A. After that point, I got in my car and started canvassing the area around Valley Place, which is where the owner of that vehicle resides.

Q. Now before you actually did that, did you have an opportunity to talk to anyone else that lived at 1435?
A. Not at that point, no.
Q. Did you have an opportunity at any point to talk to anyone else that lived in 1435?
A. Yes, sir.
Q. Okay. When was that?
A. That was—after canvassing, I came back and spoke to a young little boy that lived there.
Q. Okay. Now, before we go there, did you actually respond to Valley Place?
A. I never responded directly to the house, no. I just responded to the street and started canvassing for the vehicle.
Q. Did you ever locate the vehicle?
A. Not that day, no.
Q. Let's then talk about the conversation you had with the juvenile. Do you recall what he told you?
A. Yes, sir.
Q. What did he tell you?
MM: Objection, Your Honor, to the hearsay.
The Court: It's in the full exception.
GP: The trustworthiness has already been shown. The witness is already here for cross-examination.
MM: I would just ask—
The Court: Sustained.
Direct examination by GP (continued):
Q. Did the individual, the juvenile, explain to you what happened?
A. Yes, sir.
Q. And based upon what he told you, did you develop a suspect?
A. Yes, sir.
Q. And what was that suspect's name?
A. The individual actually told me his name was HP. That's the only thing he could remember. I asked if he had a last name. He said he didn't remember it.
Q. All right. So you had the information on HP?
A. Yes.

Q. What, if anything, did you do with that information?
A. I'm pretty sure I voiced that across the air.
Q. Did you also voice information regarding the vehicle lookout?
A. Yes, sir.
Q. What occurred with respect to MPD's further investigation of these events after those facts were aired?
MM: Objection. Foundation, Your Honor.
Direct examination by GP (continued):
Q. What happened next?
The Court: Well, what—what happened—what did you do next?
The Witness: Oh, next, after I gave the—I voiced all information over the air, I raised for another burglary unit to respond over to 1362 Valley and knock on the door and set up on that house until we had detectives go over to the house.
Q. Okay. Do you recall who actually responded to 1362 Valley Place?
A. It would have been burglary unit 5, which would have been Corson and Savoy.
Q. Officers Corson and Officer—
A. Savoy, yes.
Q. Okay. And you actually did not enter into the house, correct?
A. Never stepped foot on the grounds.
GP: All right. I have no further questions. Thank you, Officer Smith.
Cross-examination by MM:
Q. Hello, Officer Smith.
A. How you doing, sir?
Q. Officer Smith, you testified that the vehicle that you were given the lookout for, the lookout description, you associated with HP, correct?
A. Yes, sir.
Q. But the vehicle that you were given the lookout for, the one that was supposedly on Good Hope Road, you didn't actually see that vehicle because you weren't there, correct?
A. You're correct.
Q. Okay. And the lookout you were given was for a black SUV, correct?
A. Yes, sir.

Q. All right. You weren't given a lookout for a particular make or model. Isn't that right?

A. Not that I remember. If it's in my notes possibly, but I don't remember, sir.

Q. And you—you never did, like, a DMV in DC, Maryland, or Virginia records check to see if any such vehicle was registered to an HP, correct?

A. No.

Q. Did you take handwritten notes as part of your investigation on Good Hope Road?

A. If I did, they should be there. But I'm unaware if I did because I was not the reporting officer.

Q. Okay. But you did complete a 251, correct?

A. I think that was done by my partner. I'm not sure. I'd have to look at the notes, sir.

Q. Let me show you what is being marked for identification as Defendant's Exhibit 2. I'm going—just going to hand it to you and ask you to leaf through it. That—that's a three-page—what they call a PD-251, correct?

A. Yes.

Q. And maybe you could help me out. Did you write the 251?

A. Yes, sir.

Q. Okay. So—but that's a form that you completed. It's also called an incident report, correct, isn't it?

A. Incident—yes.

Q. I'm sorry.

A. Incident or offense form, correct.

Q. Incident or offense form. Thank you, sir. You said you spoke with a—a little boy at that location?

A. Yes, sir.

Q. About nine years old?

A. At that time, he was probably either eight or nine. I don't remember exactly.

Q. His name was MB?

A. Yes.

Q. Okay. And where was MB when you spoke with him? And by that, I mean where in relation to the house was he?

A. He was inside the house, probably around the front door area.

Q. Okay. That—that front door leads into the living room area of that particular house, correct?

A. Yes.

Q. Okay. And you said you also encountered the homeowner when you went there, a female, correct?

A. Yes.

Q. All right. And when you were speaking with MB, do you know where the homeowner was?

A. I'm unaware. Had to be with my partner.

Q. Okay. And your partner is Officer Pulaski?

A. Yes.

Q. Right? Well, was Officer Pulaski also in the house at the same time?

A. I can't speak for her whereabouts. I'm not sure where she was at.

Q. Okay. And did you have any conversations with the homeowner?

A. No, sir.

Q. Officer, isn't it true that in your 251, the one that I just showed you, you wrote that "C1 reports that she heard a knock at the door. When C1 answered the door, S1 pointed a gun in her face and S1 and S2 kicked the door open"?

A. Yes. That's what I wrote in my note, in the incident report, yes.

Q. Okay. And that wasn't based on any conversation that you had with C1?

A. That is—that's—after the whole investigation was done and a report is taken, that it's going to encompass what I find out through my investigation, also my partner's.

Direct examination by GP:

Q. Officer Savoy, good afternoon to you.

A. Good afternoon, sir.

Q. Please tell us what your full name is and let the jury know how you spell your name.

A. Full name is Ryan Savoy.

The Court: You can pull back a little.

THE WITNESS: Oh, I'm sorry. Full name is Ryan Savoy. First name is spelled R-y-a-n, last name S-a-v-o-y.

DIRECT EXAMINATION BY GP (CONTINUED):

Q. Thank you, Officer. You work for the Metropolitan Police Department, correct?
A. Yes, sir.
Q. How long have you worked for the department?
A. A little over three years.
Q. And where do you currently work?
A. Seventh District.
Q. How long have you been at 7-D?
A. I'd say a little over two years.
Q. Did you become involved, Officer Savoy, in the investigation of a burglary and a corresponding shooting at a location in the 1400-block of Good Hope Road, Southeast, back in April of this year?
A. Yes, sir.
Q. Can you explain to the jury what your role was in that investigation?
A. From what I recall, I gained knowledge to respond to an address on Valley Place, Southeast, from the officers who were on the scene on Good Hope Road that the suspect lived at that location.
Q. Okay. Did you respond to that location?
A. Yes, sir.
Q. And by the way, did you ever respond personally to the address on Good Hope Road?
A. From what I recall, I did.
Q. Okay. And what did you do there?
A. I don't recall if I did anything. I just remember driving to that location.
Q. Okay. Did you get out of your vehicle?
A. Yes, sir.
Q. Did you go inside the home? Do you recall?
A. From what I recall, I didn't go inside the residence.
Q. Okay. Do you recall the address that you responded to on Valley Place?
A. Yes, sir.

Q. What was it?
A. 01362—62 Valley Place.
Q. Did you respond there by yourself, or did you have a partner?
A. I had a partner.
Q. What was your partner's name?
A. Officer Todd Kerson.
Q. Is that K-e-r-s-o-n?
A. Yes, sir.
Q. Close enough?
A. Yes, sir.
Q. What happened upon your arrival at 1362 Valley Place?
A. Officer Kerson went to the rear of the address, and then I went to the front of the address, and I knocked on the door to see if anyone was home.
Q. Was anyone home?
A. Yes, sir.
Q. How did you know that?
A. There was a female that answered the door.
Q. Did you ask the female anything?
A. I believe I asked her if anyone else was inside the house with her.
Q. Okay. And what did she say?
A. She said no.
Q. All right. Did you see a black SUV vehicle parked anywhere near 1362 upon your arrival?
A. I don't recall.
Q. Did you ultimately enter the house?
A. Yes, sir.
Q. And how was that made possible?
A. The female who answered the door allowed us to come inside the house.
Q. And who came inside?
A. Myself and Officer Kerson.
Q. What did you and Officer Kerson do?
A. We looked around to see if the suspect was inside.
Q. And the result of your looking inside the premises for the suspect was?

A. We didn't locate anyone else inside the residence.
Q. Can you describe how the residence was configured?
A. From what I recall, when you enter through the front door, you kind of have the living room area and the kitchen on the first level, and to the right was a flight of stairs that led up to the bedrooms.
Q. Single-family home?
A. It appeared to be, yes, sir.
Q. Did you go upstairs?
A. Yes, sir.
Q. Were you alone when you went upstairs?
A. No, sir.
Q. Were you permitted to go upstairs?
A. Yes, sir.
Q. By whom?
A. The female who answered the door.
Q. What did you observe upstairs?
A. When I went up the stairs, there was a bedroom—the first bedroom to the left, from what I recall, the door had been—the door was open, and when I looked inside, I saw a pair of purple shorts laying on the carpet of the floor in the bedroom.
Q. Did you see any other clothing items in the color purple?
A. Not that I recall.
Q. Did you ascertain who actually resided in that room?
MM: Objection, Your Honor, as to hearsay.
The Court: Sustained as to that, unless he saw somebody there.
Direct examination by GP (continued):
Q. What, if anything, did you do after you observed the purple shorts in the bedroom?
A. I just made a mental note of it. And I know Detective Bolding was on the scene, and I know he had become aware of it.
Q. Okay. Did there come a time when a search warrant was executed on that particular day?
A. No, sir.
Q. So what did you do—well, when did Detective Bolding arrive?
A. He arrived a short time—

Q. Detective Bolding?

A. He—he arrived a short time after myself and Officer Korsen entered through the—came—came inside the residence.

Q. And what did you see Detective Bolding do?

A. He was interviewing the female who answered the door.

Q. Did anyone raise the topic of a search warrant in your presence?

MM: Objection. Relevance, Your Honor.

THE COURT: Overruled.

A. Um, from what I recall, myself and Officer Korsen, we were advised to secure the perimeter of the house and that an emergency search warrant was to be obtained.

Q. Was that emergency search warrant obtained during your presence in the house?

A. No, sir.

GP: Court's indulgence. No further questions. Thank you, Officer.

MM: Thank you, Your Honor.

CROSS-EXAMINATION BY MM:

Q. Hello, Officer Savoy.

A. How are you doing, sir?

Q. Officer Savoy, were you—were you part of what they call the burglary 5 team?

A. I was burglary suppression unit, I believe, at that time. Our call sign has changed since then.

Q. All right. But you got a call to go over to 1362 Valley in connection with something that had—had happened just prior on Good Hope Road, correct?

A. Yes, sir.

Q. Okay. And how much time elapsed between the time you got the call to go over to Valley and the time you actually got to Valley?

A. I'd say maybe ten to fifteen minutes.

Q. Okay. And when you got there, you didn't see a black SUV at that location, correct?

A. From what I recall, no, sir, I didn't.

Q. And you were—you asked for permission to go in the house, and you were given permission, correct?

A. Yes, sir.

Q. And—and you went up and looked in one of the bedrooms, and you saw a pair of purple shorts, correct?
A. Yes, sir.
Q. And there was nobody in the bedroom, correct?
A. Correct.
Q. You see the guy to my right in the yellow shirt?
A. Yes, sir, I see him.
Q. Did you see him there?
A. No, sir.
MM: Okay. Thank you.
GP: No further questions.
THE COURT: Thank you. You may step down, Officer Savoy.
(Witness excused.)
GP: Government calls Detective Justin Bolding.
THE COURT: This will be our last witness of the day, ladies and gentlemen. Up here, Detective.
THE WITNESS: Good afternoon.
MM: Could I have the Court's indulgence to speak with GP just for a second?
THE COURT: Um-hmmm.
(Thereupon, Justin Bolding, having been called as a witness on behalf of the Government and having been first duly sworn by the deputy clerk, was examined and testified.)
DIRECT EXAMINATION BY GP:
Q. Detective Bolding, good afternoon.
A. Good afternoon.
Q. Detective, please introduce yourself to the ladies and gentlemen of the jury.
A. Detective Justin Bolding, Metropolitan Police Department. Last name Bolding, B-o-l-d-i-n-g.
Q. Detective, you work for the Metropolitan Police Department, right?
A. Correct.
Q. And how long have you been there?
A. Metropolitan Police Department for six years.
Q. What's your current rank and duty assignment?

A. I'm a detective assigned to the criminal investigations division, the Seventh District.
Q. And how long have you served as a detective?
A. I've been a detective for two years.
Q. Does your assignment encompass the 1300-block of Valley Place, Southeast?
A. Yes, it does.
Q. Did you have an opportunity to respond to that address in connection with an investigation of a burglary on April 27 of this year?
A. Yes, I did.
Q. Why were you asked to respond to that location?
A. I was called to the location by patrol officers who stated that they had—
MM: Objection to the hearsay, Your Honor.
The Court: Well, I'll allow it to explain this on the detective's subsequent actions, not for the truth.
The Witness: I was called to the location by patrol officers to assist in an investigation in reference to a burglary. I was called to the house because I was told by an officer that the house is the residence of—
MM: Same objection.
The Court: Ladies and gentlemen, obviously he—he has no personal knowledge of whether that fact is true or not, and so it's not offered for its truth. It's only offered to explain what he was told and why he did what he did.
GP: Thank you, Your Honor.
Direct examination by GP (continued):
Q. Did you actually respond to that address?
A. Yes. Yes, I did.
Q. Okay. In terms of police officers, who, if anyone, was present when you got there?
A. I believe it was Officer Savoy, um, Officer—
Q. How many officers? It was approximately two officers in the house and two or three officers standing outside of the home?
A. Yes.

Q. Did you enter the home?
A. Yes, I did.
Q. What did you do when you went inside?
A. I spoke to a young lady who stated that she lived inside of the home.
Q. Did the person that you spoke to permit you to look around inside the house?
A. Yes, she did.
Q. And what did you do?
A. I walked upstairs, and I looked around the upstairs living quarters and the bathroom area of the house.
Q. And did you look inside any bedrooms of the house?
A. Two of the bedrooms inside the house were locked with a deadbolt from the outside. One of the bedrooms was open with the deadbolt lock open, still hanging on the outside door. I didn't enter the room, but from the outside of the room, I did look inside.
Q. What, if anything, did you see?
A. It was a normal bedroom, you know, TV, bed. On the floor, hanging halfway inside the room and halfway in the hallway area, were a pair of purple shorts.
Q. Did those purple shorts have any meaning to you as far as your investigation was concerned?
A. Yes, sir.
Q. What was that?
MM: Objection, Your Honor.
The Court: Again, ladies and gentlemen, this statement is not offered for its truth, only to explain what this detective did.
Direct examination by GP (continued):
Q. Go ahead.
A. Purple shorts were given in a lookout broadcast over the air after the burglary.
Q. Did you seize those shorts?
A. I didn't seize the shorts at that time. No, I did not.
Q. Why not?

A. We wanted to obtain a search warrant to be able to look around the entire home and also seize any property.
Q. Was that search warrant obtained?
A. Yes.
Q. That day?
A. I'm not—I believe it wasn't, but I wasn't the one that applied for it.
Q. Were you present when the search warrant was actually executed?
A. No, I was not.
GP: Court's indulgence. No further questions. Thank you, Detective.
Cross-examination by MM:
Q. Hello, Detective.
A. Good afternoon.
Q. Detective, when you got to 1362 Valley, was Officer Savoy already there?
A. Yes, sir.
MM: Okay. Thanks.
GP: No further questions.
The Court: Thank you, Detective. You may step down.
The Witness: Thank you.
(Witness excused.)
The Court: That completes the testimony for today?
GP: Yes.
The Court: Ladies and gentlemen, that completes the testimony for today. It's a little early, but that just means we're going quicker than the lawyers expected, which is good. So, as I indicated, we're going to have you back on Monday morning. Now, there are going to be some changes. This is Superior Court. There are always changes. So the Court is in a process of—we have to—behind each courtroom is a cellblock, and the doors don't always work.

So they are remodeling the cellblocks in each of these courtrooms. And on Monday, it's scheduled for this courtroom. It was independent of this case. It was a regular schedule. And so they just did that courtroom last week. They're doing this courtroom. So we will be moved down to courtroom 101. Mr. Phillips is going to take you down there now just so that you can eyeball it and see it. But you won't be reporting to this courtroom; you'll be reporting to courtroom 101, and that's where we'll continue the case. We think the case is on schedule, assuming everybody shows up and, you know, it's good weather and all that.

So over the course of the weekend, do not discuss the case among yourselves or with anyone else. Don't go to this area to try to do your own investigation. Don't go on social media to discuss the case, and don't go on the internet to investigate the case. So we'll see you tomorrow morning at—

THE JUROR: Tomorrow or Monday?

THE COURT: Monday. Thank you. Thank you very much. Monday at—I'm going to have you come in at 11:30. I might have to do two calendars on Monday because it's a judge—never mind. So I'm going to have you come in at 11:30. I don't think it's going to hold up the case. But as you can see, when you come to court, some things unexpected happen. Things don't always work on time. So you sort of have to build that into your travel time, so if you can keep that in mind on Monday. We'll see you on Monday. Thank you very much. Have a good weekend.

THE JURY: Thank you.

(Jury out.)

THE COURT: Do you mind if we—we go on tape at this point so I can release the court reporter?

MM: Yes, Your Honor.

THE COURT: Thank you.

(Proceedings adjourned at approximately 4:38 p.m.)

Certificate of Reporter

I, Kristin Gilliam, an Official Court Reporter for the Superior Court of the District of Columbia, do hereby certify that I reported, by machine shorthand, in my official capacity, the proceedings had and testimony adduced upon the jury trial in the case of the *UNITED STATES OF AMERICA versus HP*, Criminal Action Number 2011-CF3-8205, in said court on the thirteenth day of October, 2011.

I further certify that the foregoing 195 pages constitute the official transcript of said proceedings, as taken from my machine shorthand notes, together with the backup tape of said proceedings to the best of my ability.

In witness whereof, I have hereto subscribed my name, this the twenty-ninth day of March, 2012.

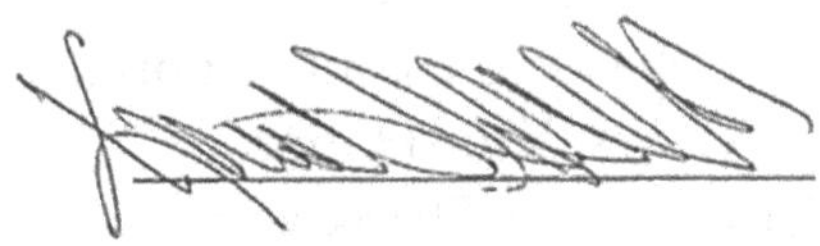

Kristi Gilliam
Official Court Reporter

Superior Court of the District of Columbia
Criminal Division
United States of America vs. HP, Defendant
Criminal Action Number 2011-CF3-8205
Washington, DC
Wednesday, October 19, 2011

The above-entitled matter came on for a trial before the Honorable Robert E. Morin, Associate Judge, and a jury in the Courtroom Number 312, commencing at approximately 10:30 a.m.

This transcript represents the product of an official reporter, engaged by the court, who has personally certified that it represents testimony and proceedings of the case as recorded.

Appearances:

On behalf of the Government: GP, Esquire, Assistant United States Attorney

On behalf of the Defendant: MM, Esquire, Washington, DC

Gercha Richards White
(202) 879-1087
Official Court Reporter

PROCEEDINGS

THE DEPUTY CLERK: Calling from Your Honor's trial calendar, *United States v. HP*, 2011 CF3-8205.

MM: MM for HP, Your Honor.

THE COURT: Get GP.

(Pause.)

THE DEPUTY CLERK: GP, can you hear us okay?

GP: I can hear.

THE DEPUTY CLERK: We're just waiting for the defendant, GP, in case you're wondering what's going on.

GP: No problem.

(Pause.)

THE COURT: HP now is in the present. We received a note from the jury as follows: "What is the definition of assault, from number 3, first-degree burglary while unarmed?" Can you hear me, GP?

GP: Yes.

THE COURT: Okay. Received a note which indicates: "Please define assault from number 3 in first-degree burglary while unarmed."

I'm prepared to answer as follows: For the definition of *assault*, please refer to Elements A1 through 3 and B1 through 3 under "Assault with a Dangerous Weapon" on pages 7 and 8 of the instructions. Any objection to that?

GP: Okay.

THE COURT: GP, any objection?

GP: No objection.

THE COURT: MM?

MM: None, Your Honor.

THE COURT: Okay. Thank you. That will be submitted, written—written answer to the jury.

MM: Very well, Your Honor.

THE COURT: Thank you for appearing. Thank you, GP.

GP: Thank you, Your Honor.

THE DEPUTY CLERK: Thank you, GP.

(A break was taken.)

THE DEPUTY CLERK: On Your Honor's file calendar *United States v. HP*, Case Number 2011 CF3-8205.

GP: Good afternoon, Your Honor. GP for the United States.

MM: Good afternoon, Your Honor. MM for HP, who's on his way out.

(Pause.)

THE COURT: HP's present.

We received two notes. The first note is "Can we get the written transcript of MB and KW's conversation pages that were called in the trial?" I don't know your views on that.

MM: My view is it wasn't admitted, it goes back. But I think they should be allowed to even rehear the interview or in the jury box. I could certainly hand out the transcripts or do both.

THE COURT: That is true. We would have the right to replay it, so it's up to you. It's your call.

GP: That's fine, Your Honor.

THE COURT: Sending the transcript, or do you want to do it here or send it back? It's up to you, either way.

GP: I'd rather replay it.

THE COURT: Okay. So tell them to play it at 2:15.

The second one is "Did the charges include events throughout today or just the event when 911 was called?"

GP: It would be, I suppose I—I have to think about that.

THE COURT: I think what the—I think a reasonable inference is they're trying to determine the first event, which is arguably one event is the charged event or whether—

GP: It would be—it would be the average.

THE COURT: Okay. So how do you want me to answer? It would be the events that occurred right before the 911 call?

GP: That's right. That gave rise to the 911 call.

MM: Or related to the 911 call and not any events that may have occurred prior to that, I would suggest.

THE COURT: Make it real simple.

So I'm going to answer in writing: "The charges apply to the event that occurred right before and which gave rise to the 911 call," and tell them the clerk will instruct them after lunch at 2:15 to listen to the transcript.

Now, let me advise the parties about an event that was brought to my attention. We received a—the clerk received the box of evidence, submitted it to the jury; the jury knocked on the door later in the morning and discovered a bullet from 13—what was the address—1362 Valley Place and asked the clerk whether or not this was evidence, since it didn't have an evidence sticker on it. They were told it was not, and it was returned.

MM: Was the bullet in a bag, Your Honor, that was marked?

THE COURT: It was in a plastic bag.

MM: I assume the plastic bag had the markings.

THE COURT: Correct. I'm assuming, too. That's the jury's inquiry.

MM: I'd like to discuss that matter with my client, if I may, Your Honor.

THE COURT: Right. Now, if—I don't know whether the jury asked a question about the lesser included, which would make the portion of the offense—well—

MM: My concern is just that if they've seen that and they know it was in evidence and did the right thing, obviously letting the clerk know, but that they may be connecting that to the events that happened before; or some person in the jury caused to think there was a bullet there, this person has access to a gun.

THE COURT: Here's what's under consideration. We're coming back at 2:15 to listen to the tapes. If you want me to give a cautionary instruction at that time, that it wasn't in evidence in this case and was accidentally placed there, then you don't have to consider it in any way. I would be glad to give any kind of cautionary instruction.

MM: There are other options. I'll discuss it with my client.

The Court: Those other options just for your purpose are likely to be taken under advisement and then—so I'm actually discussing a plan B option.

MM: I see what you're saying. Defense was asking for a mistrial, but Your Honor would obviously preserve.

The Court: Correct.

MM: I understand.

The Court: If you have a cautionary instruction you propose, I'm sure GP won't be objecting to it as well. If you come up with others, that will be fine.

GP: I'll discuss it with my client.

The Court: Thank you. I'll see you at 2:15.

(A luncheon recess was taken at 1:05 p.m.)

Afternoon Session

(Back on the record at 2:17 p.m.)

The Deputy Clerk: Calling from Your Honor's trial calendar *United States v. HP*, Case Number 2011 CF3-8205.

GP: Good afternoon, Your Honor. GP with the United States.

MM: Good afternoon, Your Honor. MM for HP, who's present.

The Court: MM.

MM: So we address the—

The Court: Yes.

MM: Very well. HP is going to ask the Court for a mistrial, Your Honor, and I understand Your Honor's inclination to observe. Would Your Honor like to hear my reasons?

The Court: I'll reserve.

MM: Very well.

The Court: Any other alternative?

MM: Good afternoon, Your—

MM: I do. In the alternative, we'll ask for instruction, and the parties have agreed on.

The Court: If I could just see the writing.

(Pause.)

The Court: Okay. I'll read that for the jury.

MM: Before Your Honor brings the jury out—

The Court: Sure. Well, I'll ask the clerk to assemble the jury while you're doing that. Just let us know when you're ready.

Just put the transcripts on each, 7 and 8 are not—

MM: Oh, yeah. Here's 1, 2, and 3 are 2—

(Pause.)

The Court: You're going to investigate how that happened.

GP: Yeah, I will. I'm sure I have a handle as to what happened.

The Court: Stuff happens. Make sure the other jury doesn't come into the room while we're doing this.

The Marshal: Yes, sir.

The Court: Thanks so much, sir.

The Deputy Clerk: The jury would like to know if they're allowed to bring their notebook or not.

The Court: Yes. Okay.

(Jury in at 2:22 p.m.)

The Court: Good afternoon, ladies and gentlemen. Before we begin, let me give you an instruction. Ladies and gentlemen, it has come to my attention that earlier today, a bullet was erroneously sent back to you along with all the evidence. We instructed that the bullet is not evidence in this case, and you should disregard it when deliberating about the case.

Ladies and gentlemen, we've provided transcripts, now the tapes will be played.

MM: Thank you, Your Honor.

The Court: Can you just indicate to the jury which transcript you'll be looking at first?

MM: Certainly. There are three clips.

The first is marked Clip 1, and you should have a transcript for Clip 1, Clip 2, Clip 3, and 3A, and I'm going to play Clip 1 now.

(Playing Clip 1.)

MM: The jury—I'm now going to play as marked on the transcript as Clip Number 2.

(Playing Clip 2.)

MM: Now, for the jury, the transcript that is marked Clip 3A.

(Playing Clip 3A.)

MM: I'm going to back it up a little bit.

The Deputy Clerk: Move it away from the microphone.

The Court: There you go.

(Playing Clip 3A.)

The Court: Any member of the jury wish any portion to be played again? If you could pass the transcripts down to one side.

Thank you. You may resume your deliberations.

The Jurors: Thank you.

(Jury out at 2:27 p.m.)

MM: Excuse for now, Your Honor.

The Court: Thanks so much.

GP: Thank you, Your Honor.

(A break was taken.)

(Jury in at 3:13 p.m.)

The Court: Good afternoon, ladies and gentlemen. We've received a note that you've reached a verdict. At this time, the Court will take the verdict. Will the foreperson please stand and give us the last three numbers of your juror number?

The Foreperson: 174.

The Court: Mr. Foreperson, speaking on behalf of the jury, has the jury reached a unanimous verdict as to each count?

The Foreperson: Yes, sir.

The Court: As to the charge of first-degree burglary while armed, how do you find the defendant: not guilty or guilty?

The Foreperson: Not guilty.

The Court: As to the lesser included charge of first-degree burglary unarmed, how did you find the defendant: not guilty or guilty?

The Foreperson: Guilty.

The Court: And am I correct, Mr. Foreperson, as a matter of law, you found the defendant not guilty of possession of a firearm during the crime of first-degree burglary while armed?

The Foreperson: Yes, sir.

The Court: As to the charge of assault with a dangerous weapon, how did you find the defendant: not guilty or guilty?

The Foreperson: Not guilty.

THE COURT: Am I correct, Mr. Foreperson, that as a matter of law, you found the defendant not guilty of possession of a firearm during the assault with a dangerous weapon?

THE FOREPERSON: Yes, sir.

THE COURT: As to the charge of carrying a pistol without a license, how do you find the defendant: not guilty or guilty?

THE FOREPERSON: Not guilty.

THE COURT: As to the charge of possession of ammunition, how did you find the defendant: not guilty or guilty?

THE FOREPERSON: Not guilty.

THE COURT: As to the charge of destruction of property of the front door, how did you find the defendant—

THE FOREPERSON: Not guilty.

THE COURT::—not guilty or guilty?

THE FOREPERSON: I'm sorry. Not guilty.

THE COURT: All right. Ladies and gentlemen, the foreperson has announced that you found the defendant guilty of first-degree burglary unarmed and not guilty of each and every other charge. Do each of you agree?

THE JURORS: Yes.

THE COURT: You may be seated.

Ladies and gentlemen, I'm going to engage in what's called the poll of the jury. I'm going to ask each individual juror by seat number whether you agree with all the verdicts as announced by your foreperson. If you agree with all the verdicts as announced by your foreperson, please state that you agree. If you disagree with any verdict as announced by your foreperson, please state you disagree. Juror in seat number 1, do you agree or disagree?

THE JUROR: I agree.

THE COURT: Juror in seat number 2, do you agree or disagree?

THE JUROR: I agree.

THE COURT: Juror in seat number 3, do you agree or disagree?

THE JUROR: Agree.

THE COURT: Juror in seat number 4, do you agree or disagree?

THE JUROR: I agree.

THE COURT: Juror in seat number 5, do you agree or disagree?

THE JUROR: I agree.

THE COURT: Juror in seat number 6, do you agree or disagree?

THE JUROR: I agree.

THE COURT: Juror in seat number 9, do you agree or disagree?

THE JUROR: I agree.

THE COURT: Juror in seat number 10, do you agree or disagree?

THE JUROR: I agree.

THE COURT: Juror in seat number 11, do you agree or disagree?

THE JUROR: I agree.

THE COURT: Juror in seat number 12, do you agree or disagree?

THE JUROR: I agree.

THE COURT: Juror in seat number 13, do you agree or disagree?

THE JUROR: I agree.

THE COURT: Juror in seat number 14, do you agree or disagree?

THE JUROR: I agree.

THE COURT: Any additional requests?

MM: Not from the defense.

THE COURT: Ladies and gentlemen, with your polling, that does conclude your service in this matter. On behalf of the Court and the community, we thank you for resolving this matter. I'm not sure I've felt a jury who's gotten along as well as you all have with each other. We do appreciate the time that you put into it.

You are free to discuss this case with anyone at this point. You're also free not to discuss the case with anyone. It's totally up to you whether you wish to discuss the case or whom you wish to discuss it with. We're going to ask that you be excused out to the jury office on the third floor, and with the Court's thanks, you're excused at this time. We'll see you in a couple of years.

If you could provide the verdict to the clerk. Thanks very much. Is it signed and dated? Make sure.

THE DEPUTY CLERK: It is.

(Jury out at 3:16 p.m.)

THE COURT: Okay. All right. Will we be proceeding on the remaining charge or—

GP: No, Your Honor.

THE COURT: Okay. Thank you.

So the possession of the firearm felon will be dismissed. I guess I'll hear you at this point on the motion for mistrial since there was no conviction on any armed matter.

MM: I think it weakens the argument, Your Honor, but not necessarily—it eliminates the prejudice. The bullet was found at 1362 coincidentally when JH called JH to the trial, said that there had been an encounter with NW, who, in fact, was putting a laser-guided gun to his head right at that location, and it was also NW, according to some testimony in the case, that was the other person who was accompanying HP to the location. So a bullet at that location tied to NW—I guess, somewhat in a prejudicial way—ties HP to NW.

The Court: GP, first, were you able to determine how that item was placed in the evidence box?

GP: I was not—have not had a chance to talk to the officer.

The Court: Do you have any indication that it was intentionally done?

GP: That's exactly what I was about to address, Your Honor. Yesterday, before the evidence was sent back to the jury, we took an opportunity, Counsel and I, together, to go through all the elements. We separated all that which was not admitted, including a couple of cameras, the bullet, and some miscellaneous hangers and things, and we put all of that property in a plastic bag and set it aside. Then what went back was the clothing and shell casing.

I gave the box and the bag to the crime scene search officer, who then left. Came back this morning with one box, which I presumed did not include the plastic bag with separated property. So from yesterday until this morning, somehow the plastic bag material got mixed with the clothing and the shell casings. That's my theory.

The Court: Surmise.

GP: Yeah. I haven't confirmed that, but the bottom line, Your Honor: it certainly wasn't done in bad faith—would be the Government's position.

The Court: Well, I can reserve on this until GP does further investigation. Let me just make a couple of observations that may influence the Court's decision. Number 1, it was a juror who brought to the clerk's attention that it wasn't evidence and identified it, as returned to the clerk, and I believe the clerk reported that when the juror passed it over, so we're not going to consider it since it's not evidence—that was the spontaneous statement. Am I correct in that?

THE DEPUTY CLERK: Yes.

THE COURT: Spontaneous statement made by the juror.

Secondly, we did give a curative instruction, again reemphasizing that they weren't to consider it. And finally, I might have been more concerned if there was any conviction on any weapon-related offense, but there was no conviction on that. I think a fair inference is that the jury concluded that the defendant had no connection with any firearm used or not used during this event. So my tentative view would be that the defense has not suffered any prejudice by the mistaken inclusion of a single bullet in a plastic bag, and the jury was instructed not to consider it. I'm going to let GP conclude his investigation to make sure he can make further representations.

Just for the clerk's edification, I think the Government dismissed the remaining felon possession as well as the lawful ammunition for the purposes of the docket entry.

GP: Your Honor, I'm going to order a presentence report for the presentencing day.

THE COURT: Am I correct—plea up to this case?

GP: Yes, exactly. It's a long plea offer, I guess.

MM: Is it six or eight weeks?

THE COURT: I think it's eight weeks. Would be in January.

THE DEPUTY CLERK: In January.

MM: I'm available in the first week of January, anytime.

THE COURT: I think we're open. Obviously, that Friday will probably be jam-packed. It's my first day back.

MM: The first week is not open?

THE COURT: It is open, just that Friday usually, historically, is a crowded day.

MM: Oh, I see. Well, I'm available Monday, Tuesday, Wednesday, or Thursday.

The Court: Okay. How about that Thursday?

The Deputy Clerk: The fifth.

GP: That's a good day.

The Court: Thank you. And you could submit a memorandum to the extent you can make representations.

Thank you, GP.

GP: Thank you.

The Court: Thank you, MM.

MM: Thank you.

(Proceedings were concluded at 3:23 p.m.)

Certificate of Reporter

I, Gercha Richards White, an Official Court Reporter for the Superior Court of the District of Columbia, do hereby certify that I reported, by machine shorthand, in my official capacity, the proceedings had and testimony adduced upon the jury trial in the case of the *UNITED STATES OF AMERICA versus HP*, Criminal Action Number 2011 CF3-8205, in said court on the 19th day of October, 2011.

I further certify that the foregoing 20 pages constitute the official transcript of said proceedings, as taken from my machine shorthand notes, together with the backup tape of said proceedings to the best of my ability.

IN WITNESS WHEREOF, I have hereunto subscribed my name, this 30th day of April, 2012.

Gercha Richards White
Official Court Reporter

Superior Court of the District of Columbia
Criminal Division
United States of America vs. HP, Defendant
Criminal Action Number 2011 CF3-8205
Washington, DC
Monday, October 17, 2011

The above-entitled matter came on for a trial before the Honorable Robert E. Morin, Associate Judge, and a jury in the Courtroom Number commencing at approximately 11:42 a.m.

This transcript represents the product of an official reporter, engaged by the court, who has personally certified that it represents testimony and proceedings of the case as recorded.

Appearances:
On behalf of the Government: GP Esquire
On behalf of the Defendant: MM, Esquire, Washington, DC

Gercha Richards White
(202) 879-1087
Official Court Reporter

PROCEEDINGS

THE DEPUTY CLERK: Calling from Your Honor's trial calendar, *United States v. HP*, 2011 CF3-8205.

(Pause.)

THE COURT: I'm working through your instruction request, so I'll work through that. I think obviously you'll have to—the evidence is not closed, but I think I will hear argument on self-defense.

MM: Very well, Your Honor.

THE COURT: And is the Government opposing the lesser included—

GP: No.

THE COURT: On a—

GP: No, we are not, Your Honor.

THE COURT: All right. Thank you. Are there any preliminary matters?

GP: There is actually a potential matter that I'm not quite sure how to handle, but I think we need to approach, Your Honor.

THE COURT: Okay. Surely.

(Bench conference.)

THE COURT: Good morning.

GP: Good morning. Judge, there was a potential defense witness by the name of Detective Rodney Hollins. The Government had considered calling Detective Hollins, but we, for a couple of reasons, decided against it. One of the reasons is that he happens to be on the Lewis list. Now, I don't know if the Court is aware—

THE COURT: Refresh my memory.

GP: He was engaged in litigation with his brother, civil litigation, regarding the execution of his father's estate and a four-unit apartment building in the city. There was a lot of rancor between the two men, which caused the brother to make some allegations against Detective Hollins. The brother ended up going to Internal Affairs of the Police Department, making an allegation that his brother told some untruths during the litigation of the civil action, so they needed to know about it. The bottom line is he was exonerated by the Adverse Action Panel of MPD, and I have the conclusions here. They essentially said there's no basis to any of this, and Detective Hollins is not guilty. So, while it's the Government's position that there is no substance to this Lewis situation, we felt that it was appropriate to at least advise the Court in the event that the defense calls him as a witness.

THE COURT: How would it arise if the defense called him as a witness?

MM: I don't know that it would. May I ask a question, Your Honor, of GP?

THE COURT: Yes.

MM: This litigation is over at the board?

GP: Yes.

MM: But the litigation with the brother is not?

GP: That I'm not aware of, but certainly whatever conclusions the board came up with are contained here and are fine.

THE COURT: I'm going to assume that it's not going to come up, frankly, because I don't think—

MM: I think Your Honor can reserve on it, and if it's an issue for the defense, I'll raise it.

THE COURT: Right. But in general, for the defense to call a witness and then to attack that witness's bias is kind of a—so that's why I'm assuming it's not going to come up. Unless you think it's going to arise during a question, you'll have to approach the bench before it's raised.

MM: I would say it's possible it would come up, but not likely.

THE COURT: Okay.

MM: We'll just leave it at that. Okay. Thank you.

(Open court.)

THE COURT: Ready for the jury.

(Jury in at 11:50 a.m.)

THE COURT: Good morning, ladies and gentlemen. Hope you had a good weekend. We're still in the Government's case, so the Government may call its next witness.

GP: Thank you, Your Honor. Good morning, ladies and gentlemen. At this time, the Government calls Crime Scene Officer Erin Price.

(Therefore, Erin Price, having been called as a witness on behalf of the Government and having been first duly sworn by the deputy clerk, was examined and testified.)

DIRECT EXAMINATION BY GP:

Q. Ms. Price, good morning.

A. Good morning.

Q. How are you today?

A. Good.

Q. Excellent. Ms. Price, please do me the favor of introducing yourself to the ladies and gentlemen of this jury by stating and spelling your name.

A. My name is Erin Price, E-r-i-n P-r-i-c-e.

Q. Can you pull that microphone down a little bit?

(Witness complies.)

GP: Thank you.

Q. Ms. Price, you work for the Metropolitan Police Department, correct?

A. Correct.

Q. What is it that you do there?

A. I'm a crime scene technician.

Q. And how long have you served as a crime scene technician?

A. Approximately two and a half years.

Q. And what is your complete duration with the Metropolitan Police Department?

A. Two years and three months.

Q. Okay. What is a crime scene technician?

A. A crime scene technician basically is an individual who responds to crime scenes. Once we get to the crime scene, we identify evidence, collect evidence, process evidence, and then prepare reports on our findings.

Q. Okay. And once you respond to a particular location, is there a rule upon which you follow that dictates what you do? In other words, when you respond to a scene, are there certain things that you intend to accomplish?
A. Yes.
Q. At a crime scene?
A. Yes.
Q. And what is that?
A. Basically, when I first get there, I want to talk to the first responding officer to get the details of the crime scene, what they came upon, so I get an idea of what I'm walking into. And then once I do that, I actually go and do a walk-through, and then I take photos. Depending on what is in the crime scene, that would determine what other processes I need to take.
Q. Okay. Very good. I'd like to direct your attention to April 27 of this year. Did you have an opportunity to respond to a house, a single-family house, located at 1435 Good Hope Road?
A. Yes, I did.
Q. And what was the purpose of your responding to that house?
A. I was called for a burglary 1.
Q. Did you respond to the house alone, or did you have a partner that particular day?
A. I had a technician assisting me, yes.
Q. Okay. Can you explain to the ladies and gentlemen of the jury what you did when you got there?
A. Once I got to the scene, I talked to Officer Pulaski, I believe, who was the lead officer, to get the details of the crime scene. Once I got the details, we did a walk-through. My assisting technician took photographs of the scene while I identified the evidence. After identifying the evidence, we diagrammed it and then collected it.
Q. Can you give us a general idea of the configuration of this house located at 1435 Good Hope Road?
A. It was a two-story house. The main floor, I believe, was just the living room. There's a staircase in the living room that goes up to the second floor, and there's also an attic.

GP: Court's indulgence.

Direct examination by GP (continued):

Q. Did you recover any evidence?

A. Yes, I did.

Q. What did you recover?

A. Four shell casings.

Q. I'd like to show you, if I could, Officer Price, a few photographs. Let me know if you recognize what these are. First of all, I'll show you what has already been admitted into evidence as Government's Exhibit 15. What is Government's Exhibit 15?

MM: May I reposition, Your Honor?

The Witness: Okay. This is the address where I responded, 1435 Good Hope Road.

Direct examination by GP (continued):

Q. Okay. And again, showing you another exhibit that has been admitted into evidence previously, which is Government's Exhibit 16. What is Government's Exhibit 16?

A. That is the front door of the residence I responded to.

Q. I'm showing you what has not been admitted into evidence but has been shown to defense counsel, Number 17. What is Number 17?

A. That is the staircase from the first floor going up to the second floor of the residence.

Q. I'm showing you 18. What is that?

A. That is a further photograph of the stairs going up to the second floor of the residence.

Q. Number 20?

A. That is a suspected bullet hole in the wall at the top of the staircase.

Q. Okay. The top of the staircase, which is reflected in Number 18?

A. Correct.

Q. Okay. Number 21?

A. That is the top of the staircase leading to the attic of the residence.

Q. And how is the attic accessed?

A. From the bedroom on the second floor.

Q. Number 19?

A. That is the landing of the staircase going up to the second floor.

Q. Okay. Where would that bullet hole be in reference to Number 19?
A. It would be up on the wall, like on the top of this wall right here (*indicating*).
Q. And you're pointing to the upper left-hand corner of the photograph?
A. Yes.
Q. Number 22, Officer, what is that?
A. That is the front door of the residence, an up-close picture showing damage to the front door.
Q. Okay. Number 23?
A. That is one of the shell casings we found in one of the bedrooms of the residence.
Q. And what is the number 3 placard? What is its significance?
A. That is indicating item number 3.
Q. And 24?
A. That is another shell casing we found in one of the bedrooms of the residence.
GP: I move for the admission of 24, 23, 19, 21, 18, 20, and 17, Your Honor.
The Court: Be admitted.
(Government's Exhibit Numbers 24, 23, 19, 21, 18, 20, and 17 are admitted into evidence.)
GP: Thank you.
Direct examination by GP (continued):
Q. Showing you now Government's Exhibit 30. What is Government's Exhibit 30, Officer Price?
A. This is the diagram of the second floor of the residence at 1435 Good Hope Road.
Q. Can you point to the bedroom in which the attic is accessed?
A. Yes, I can. This bedroom right here (*indicating*).
Q. You're pointing to what has been marked on the diagram as the northeast bedroom, correct?
A. Correct.
Q. And is there any designation on this exhibit as to where the shell casings you mentioned were recovered?

A. Yes. My measurements are on the diagram.
Q. Okay. And can you point out which numbers—I see they're numbered and circled on the diagram?
A. Yes.
Q. What are those numbers circled?
A. The numbers circled are the items of evidence, including the shell casings we found in the bedroom.
Q. Okay. So item number 1 would be what?
A. Item number 1 is a shell casing.
Q. And item number 2?
A. Shell casing.
Q. 3?
A. Shell casing.
Q. 4?
A. Shell casing.
Q. And what's the relation between the location where the shell casings were recovered and the entry to the attic?
A. Items numbers 1 and 2 were right next to the entrance of the stairwell to the attic, and items 3 and 4 were in the bedroom, close to the door.
Q. Okay. Showing you Government's 1, 2, 3, and 4, Officer Price, what are those?
A. These are the shell casings that I collected at 1435 Good Hope Road.
Q. And how do you know those are the same shell casings?
A. They're marked with a DCN number, as well as my initials and the date when they were recovered.
Q. What is a shell casing, Officer?
A. A shell casing is basically the covering for a bullet. It's part of a cartridge. A cartridge is the bullet enclosed in the casing, and once it's fired through a gun, the bullet is extracted, and the shell casing is left.
GP: At this time, I move for the admission of Government's 1, 2, 3, and 4, Your Honor.
The Court: Be admitted.

(Government's Exhibit Numbers 1, 2, 3, and 4 are admitted into evidence.)

Direct examination by GP (continued):

Q. Did you recover any shell casings anywhere else in the house?

A. No.

Q. And by the way, what's the caliber of each one of the shell casings, if you know?

A. I would have to see.

(Witness reviews document.)

Q. Would your report refresh your recollection?

A. Yes. Yes, please.

Q. Showing you Government's 48, for purposes of refreshing your recollection. Take a look at that for me, Officer, and let me know when you're ready.

A. Okay.

Q. All right. I'll ask again, Officer, what is the caliber of Government's Exhibits 1, 2, 3, and 4?

A. .357.

Q. And are they all produced by the same manufacturer?

A. Yes.

Q. And what is that manufacturer?

A. May I see the report again?

Q. Sorry.

A. That's okay.

Q. Showing you again for purposes of refreshing your recollection, Government's 48.

A. It's Speer SIGs, S-p-e-e-r-S-I-G-s.

Q. Thank you, Officer.

GP: I have no further questions, Your Honor.

MM: May I, Your Honor?

Cross-examination by MM:

Q. Hello, Officer Price.

A. Hi.

Q. Officer Price, did I hear you say that you've been on the force like two years and three months?

A. Yes.

Q. So you went right from the academy to crime scene work?
A. I'm not an officer, I'm actually a civilian.
Q. Oh, I see.
A. Yes, so I went through training, and once I completed training, I observed other technicians. After following the other technicians, I was allowed to process crime scenes on my own.
Q. Okay. And how long was your formal training?
A. My formal training was about a month.
Q. Did it include classroom training?
A. Yes.
Q. And did that include mock crime scenes?
A. Yes.
Q. Okay. And that's what you did before you went out and worked with someone else at crime scenes?
A. Correct.
Q. How long did you work with other technicians before you were allowed to process crime scenes on your own?
A. I would say approximately two months.
Q. Okay. So is it fair to say you had about a month of formal training and then two months of on-the-job training before you processed crime scenes on your own?
A. Yes, correct.
Q. All right. And approximately a year and a half to two years of working in the field before you did this particular crime scene, correct?
A. Correct, yes.
Q. And as part of your formal and on-the-job training, you were trained to look for all evidence of criminality at the crime scene, correct?
A. Yes.
Q. To catalog it?
A. Correct.
Q. And to seize it and protect it, correct?
A. Correct.
Q. Right. And also to draw diagrams of crime scenes, correct?
A. Correct.

Q. And to the extent that you're able, you put on the diagram where the particular piece of evidence was found in relation to some other stationary object, correct?
A. Correct, yes.
Q. Did you complete the actual diagram in this case?
A. Yes.
Q. If I may, I would like to ask you a few questions about that.
A. Okay.
Q. I'm going to show you what has been entered as Government's Exhibit Number 30. Like GP did, I'm going to hold it behind your head.
A. Okay.
Q. You drew this diagram, correct?
A. Correct.
Q. And I see there are measurements in the northeast bedroom, correct?
A. Correct.
Q. And what did you use to make those measurements?
A. A measuring wheel.
Q. Is that like one of those things that looks like you're walking the dog, but it's got a roller on it?
A. Yes.
Q. Okay. And number 1, according to where I'm pointing on the upper left-hand side of the diagram, that number 1 corresponds with one of the casings that you found, correct?
A. Yes.
Q. And number 2 with another casing, correct?
A. Yes.
Q. 3 and 4, the same thing, correct?
A. Correct.
Q. And the two lines that are below the sentence that reads "stairs leading from second floor to attic," these two lines represent where the stairs are, correct?
A. Correct.
Q. And those are the stairs you were talking about that led from that bedroom up into the attic?

A. Correct.
Q. Now, were you careful when you drew the stairs such that the proportions of the width of the stairs are consistent with the width of the room?
A. No. That's why I put "not to scale" on my diagrams.
Q. Okay. Do you remember about how wide the stairs were?
A. No, I don't.
Q. Okay. Were they the same as the stairs that you saw in the photograph?
A. The same as the stairs going to the attic.
Q. The front stairs?
A. Possibly. I can't say for sure if they were or not.
Q. Okay. But what you do know for sure is that casing number 1 was three feet, seven inches from the wall, correct?
A. Not plus 1.5 inches, no.
Q. So it was a total of three feet?
A. Yes.
Q. Okay. And those markings would be true for this as well, such that number 3 was two feet from the wall?
A. Correct.
Q. And number 4 was one foot one inch from the wall, correct?
A. Yes.
Q. But numbers 3 and 4 were eight feet, four inches from the stairs themselves, correct?
A. Approximately, yes.
Q. Okay. And when you say approximately, is there a plus or minus that you use?
A. No. No. I can't say for certain that those were the exact measurements, so I say approximately.
Q. Okay. That's what you measured with your wheel, correct?
A. Correct.
Q. All right. And did you go up into the attic?
A. Yes.
Q. And you didn't find any shell casings in the attic, correct?
A. Correct.

Q. And since you did find shell casings in the northeast bedroom, that would indicate to you that someone had discharged a semiautomatic as opposed to a revolver, correct?
A. Correct.
Q. Because a revolver keeps the casings in the barrel when you fire it?
A. Correct.
Q. And a semiautomatic ejects the casings right out of the gun, correct?
A. Usually, correct.
Q. And when semiautomatics eject them, they normally eject them to the right, correct?
A. I can't testify to which direction they eject.
Q. Have you had any firearms training?
A. No.
Q. Have you ever seen a semiautomatic eject backwards toward the person who's shooting?
A. I can't say that I have seen that, but I'm not saying it's not possible.
Q. Okay. And part of your formal training in crime scene processing did not include how cartridges eject from handguns, correct?
A. Correct.
Q. All right. Now, I'm going to use your photos here. I'm going to show you what's been marked as Government's Exhibit 21. Okay?
A. Okay.
Q. Did you take this photograph?
A. No, I did not.
Q. But that is a photograph of the steps leading up to the attic, correct?
A. Correct.
Q. Okay. And you didn't find any casings on those steps, correct?
A. Correct.
Q. And you didn't find any bullet fragments on the steps, correct?
A. Correct.
Q. And you didn't find any bullets or bullet fragments in the attic, correct?
A. Correct.

Q. Did you search the attic for bullets or bullet fragments?
A. Yes.
Q. Okay. And what did you use to search the attic?
A. Just my eyes.
Q. Okay. Are there any devices that could be used to determine whether bullets had entered the wall?
A. I'm not sure if there are or not.
Q. You didn't cover that in your training, correct?
A. No.
Q. All right. And the composition of bullets is mostly lead, is that right, or do you know?
A. I don't know.
GP: Objection.
Cross-examination by MM (continued):
Q. Do you know if a metal detector would detect a bullet in a wall?
GP: Objection.
The Court: Overruled. That would seem to be within the scope.
The Witness: I cannot say. I don't know.
Cross-examination by MM (continued):
Q. Do you know what a metal jacket is with regard to a bullet?
A. Yes.
Q. And the metal jacket is the coating over the lead core of bullets, correct?
A. Correct.
Q. And there are—they're made of different alloys, isn't that correct?
A. Correct.
Q. Do you know if you can detect those metal casings using a metal detector?
A. Yes, you can.
Q. Okay. And you did not use one in this particular case to see if there were any bullets behind the walls, correct?
A. Correct.
Q. And that's also true for the rest of the house, correct?
A. Correct.
Q. Okay. And this is the front stairs, correct?
A. Correct.

Q. Okay. Does looking at the attic stairs in Government's Exhibit 21 and the front stairs in Government's Exhibit 18 refresh your recollection as to how wide those attic stairs might have been?
A. Yes.
Q. All right. About how wide were the attic stairs?
A. I can't tell you for certain. I'm sorry.
Q. Okay. And this is Government's Exhibit 20; you identified that as a suspected bullet hole, correct?
A. Correct.
Q. And just to be certain, you didn't use a metal detector on that hole to see if there was a bullet in there, correct?
A. Correct.
Q. You didn't look in there with a flashlight to see if you could spot a bullet, correct? And you didn't make the hole bigger or do anything to determine whether a bullet went through that drywall, correct?
A. Correct.
Q. The window in the bedroom in the northeast corner, where you found the casings, do you remember if that window was open or closed?
A. I don't recall.
Q. Do you know who took the photographs?
A. Excuse me?
Q. Do you know who took the photographs?
A. Yes, my technician who was assisting me.
Q. Okay. And that was—
A. TB.
Q. TB?
A. Uh-huh.
Q. Do you know what, if any, searches of the house TB did?
A. I don't know.
Q. Was she working under your direction?
A. She was working under my direction, yes.
Q. So since you didn't look for any bullets in that hole you identified as a suspected bullet hole, you're not sure that's a bullet hole, correct?

A. Correct.
Q. Isn't it true, Officer, that sometimes bullets recovered can be matched to a specific gun?
A. Correct.
Q. And also, sometimes bullets that are recovered can be matched to each other, correct?
A. Correct.
Q. That's because there's rifling on the inside of a handgun that puts distinct marks on a bullet, correct?
A. Correct.
Q. And if a bullet fragment is intact enough, you might be able to match that rifling to a particular gun, correct?
A. Possibly.
Q. And if you found multiple bullets, you might be able to match the rifling on the bullets to each other to determine if they were fired from the same gun, correct?
A. I don't know.
Q. But it wouldn't matter in this case because no bullets were recovered, right?
A. Correct.
A. Correct.
Q. And they weren't searched for, right?
A. Correct.
Q. Now, part of your crime scene training, the month you spent in formal training and the two months of on-the-job training, was devoted to fingerprints, correct?
A. Correct.
Q. Can you estimate how much time of your formal training was devoted to fingerprints?
TB: Objection.
The Court: Overruled.
The Witness: I can't give you an exact amount of time.
Q. While you were doing your formal training, not your on-the-job training, were there any workshops or labs where they showed you how to lift prints?
A. Yes.

Q. Did you have any classroom training on lifting prints?
A. Yes.
Q. Okay. You're aware that, at a crime scene, criminals often leave prints, correct?
A. Correct.
Q. It depends on the surface, right?
A. Correct.
Q. It depends on whether they're a secretor or a non-secretor, correct?
A. Right.
Q. And it depends on the nature of the touch whether they grab something or slide their hands across it, correct?
A. Correct.
Q. And truth be told, quite often, there aren't any prints, right?
A. It depends.
Q. Sometimes there are, right?
A. Correct.
Q. And forgive me for asking an obvious question, but fingerprints are unique to an individual, correct?
A. Correct. Yes.
Q. And you didn't take any prints in this particular case, correct?
A. Correct.
Q. And in particular with regard to Government's Exhibit Number 21, which you identified as the stairs leading up to the attic, you didn't take any prints on that handrail, correct?
A. There were no handprints found.
Q. Did you dust it for prints?
A. Yes.
Q. And you found no prints?
A. No prints.
Q. What about the stair up here?
A. No.
Q. Okay. No meaning?
A. No, we did not dust that.
Q. Okay. So you dusted the handrail leading up to the attic for prints, correct?
A. Yes.

Q. And found no prints?
A. Correct. None of value.
Q. Okay. Are you the one who determines whether they are of value?
A. No. We did not find any prints.
Q. Okay. So just to be clear, because I want to make sure I'm clear and I'm not explaining things wrong. I'm sorry.
A. Okay.
Q. Tell me if I'm wrong.
A. Okay.
Q. You dusted the handrail leading up to the attic for prints?
A. Correct.
Q. And it's not that you didn't find any prints of value, you didn't find any prints, correct?
A. Correct.
Q. Okay. But you did not dust the handrail that's on the front stairs, the ones that lead down to the front door, correct?
A. Correct.
Q. And I want to ask you a question, while I have this out there about this house.
A. Okay.
Q. If you go up the stairs and you turn to the right, that's the landing, correct?
A. Correct.
Q. And is there another step that you go up to get to the hallway?
A. I would have to see my photos.
Q. Okay.
A. But I'm a little confused. Like another step to get out from the landing to the hallway?
Q. Uh-huh.
A. I believe so, yes.
Q. Okay. And then the bedrooms are all on this side, correct?
A. No.
Q. They're on both sides?
A. I would have to see my diagram.
Q. Okay. Let me show that to you.
A. Okay.

Q. Remember the large diagram that I was showing you earlier?

A. Yes.

Q. Okay.

A. Okay. Now what was your question?

Q. All right. In Government's Exhibit Number 18, the photograph of the front steps, is the top of the steps that we're seeing in Government's Exhibit Number 18 where the hallway is, or is there another set of steps leading to the hallway, according to your diagram?

A. That's where the hallway—

Q. Okay. Where the hallway begins, yes?

A. Okay.

Q. And the hallway leads back to the bedrooms, correct?

A. Correct.

Q. Such that if you were standing on these steps or walking down these steps, you couldn't see into the bedroom until you got to the top of the stairs, correct?

A. Which bedroom?

Q. Any bedroom. Is there a bedroom that you can see before your head got over to the top of the stairs?

A. No.

MM: Okay. Have the Court's indulgence. I'm about finished, Your Honor.

(Pause.)

GP: Thank you, Officer.

Redirect examination by GP:

Q. Officer Prince?

A. Price.

Q. I'm sorry. Price. What's on the other side of that hole, which is depicted in Government's Exhibit 20?

A. I have no idea.

Q. Where is that hole?

A. It's at the top of the stairs in the wall.

Q. In the wall?

A. Uh-huh.

Q. Okay. What's above those steps?

A. The attic.
Q. Did you see any other defects in the wall similar to what's in Government's 20?
A. Anywhere in the house?
Q. Anywhere else in the house?
A. Not—
Q. For example, a hole like that at eye level in the house?
A. Not that I recall, no.
Q. Okay. Was this the first scene that you ever responded to where you processed a scene for a suspected bullet hole?
A. No.
Q. How many scenes have you processed with a suspected bullet hole?
A. I can't give you an exact number.
Q. More than two?
A. Yes.
Q. More than five?
A. Yes.
Q. More than ten?
A. Probably not more than ten, no.
Q. So between five and ten?
A. Correct.
Q. And how does this bullet hole—the appearance of the bullet hole—compare to the five or ten other bullet holes that you processed?
MM: Objection, Your Honor, relevance and lack of foundation for Counsel's attempt to establish.
The Court: Overruled.
The Witness: It's similar.
Redirect examination by GP (continued):
Q. Okay. Why do you suspect it's a bullet hole?
MM: Objection, Your Honor. Same objection.
The Court: Overruled.
The Witness: It's got the same shape as all the others that I've determined to be suspected bullet holes.
Redirect examination by GP (continued):

Q. Counsel asked you if it's possible to match, if you find certain pieces of firearm evidence such as a casing or bullet, if it's possible to forensically match those bullets or casings and examine them in such a way that you can match them with a particular gun. Do you remember that question?
A. Yes.
Q. Did you recover a gun in this case?
A. No.
Q. So was it possible for you to compare these shell casings to anything?
A. No.
Q. And in appearance, how similar were the four shell casings that you recovered?
A. Very similar.
Q. Okay. Are they still up there with you?
A. Yes.
Q. Take a look at them for me.
A. Okay.
Q. Are they all the same caliber?
A. Yes.
Q. All the same size?
A. Yes.
Q. All the same color?
A. Yes.
Q. All the same manufacturer?
A. Yes.
Q. You indicated that you've undergone some training in the area of latent print recovery?
A. Correct.
Q. During your training, did you learn whether, in each and every scenario, prints are recovered from any particular object? In other words, if I touch the railing of this jury box, is it always true that I leave a print?
A. No.
Q. Do you know why that is?
A. Depending on the surface, there are multiple reasons why.

Q. Okay. And if a print is left on an object, does that necessarily mean that print remains there forever?
A. No.
Q. And why not?
A. Depending on circumstances, there are many reasons why they may not remain.
Q. If you manage to recover a print of value, what would you have done?
A. I would have lifted it and then sent it to latent fingerprint.
Q. So why didn't you do that?
A. Because I found no fingerprints that I determined to be of value to lift.
Q. Thank you, Officer. I have no further questions.
The Court: Thank you, Officer. You may step down.
(Witness excused.)
The Court: Next witness, please.
GP: Timothy Ignas.
(Therefore, Timothy Ignas, having been called as a witness on behalf of the Government and having been first duly sworn by the deputy clerk, was examined and testified.)
Direct examination by GP:
Q. Officer, good morning—or good afternoon, actually.
A. Good afternoon, sir.
Q. Please introduce yourself to the ladies and gentlemen of the jury by stating and spelling your name.
A. I'm Officer Timothy Ignas, last name is spelled I-g-n-a-s.
Q. Officer Ignas, who do you work for?
A. Metropolitan Police Department.
Q. And what do you do for the Metropolitan Police Department?
A. I'm currently in the Seventh District Vice Unit.
Q. How long have you served in the Seventh District Vice Unit?
A. I've been in the Seventh District Vice Unit for approximately three years now.
Q. How long have you been a police officer with the Metropolitan Police Department?
A. Seven years.

Q. Officer, did you have an opportunity to respond to a house located at 1362 Valley Place, Southeast, in the month of April 2011?
A. Yes, sir.
Q. Do you remember what day you responded to that house?
A. It was April 27, 2011.
Q. And what was the purpose of your response?
A. We were assisting the Seventh District Detective's Office with the execution of a search warrant.
Q. What did you do when you got there?
A. My primary role that day was to photograph evidence if and when there was any evidence to be found.
Q. All right. So just so the record is clear, are you officially titled a crime scene search officer?
A. Yes.
Q. But you work out of the Seventh District?
A. Yes. We have a dedicated unit that solely concentrates on all aspects of crime scene analysis and responding to scenes. I'm not part of that. I—although I have received training in photography and taking fingerprints and such.
Q. Thank you. Again, I'm referring to 1362 Valley Place. Explain to the ladies and gentlemen what you did upon arriving there.
A. Essentially, once entry is made, officers will go throughout the property. First and foremost, safety is the primary concern. So, if anyone is in the building, they will be secured. There was no one there that day, though. After that, officers will spread out and begin looking for evidence. In this case, we had an idea of what to look for, primarily purple clothing, and any other aspects that may indicate criminal activity.
Q. Did you actually take any photographs?
A. I did.
Q. And did you actually seize any items?
A. Yes.
Q. Showing you three photographs, Officer. First is Government's Number 26. What are we looking at here?
A. This is another officer. I took this picture. He's pointing to the purple clothing in the closet.

Q. Okay. And what closet of the house are we referring to?
A. This would be—I believe it's the upstairs bedroom.
Q. Showing you Government's 27. What are we looking at here?
A. This is a purple shirt hanging off the TV in the same bedroom.
Q. And, finally, Government's 28?
A. This would be a pair of purple shorts that were on the bed in the same bedroom.
Q. Did you search any other bedrooms of the house?
A. I personally did not search. The other officers did the searching. If they found something, they would raise it for me, and then the seizing officer, usually the affiant of the warrant, would respond. I would photograph it, and the seizing officer would seize it.
Q. Were you directed to any other room of the house for purposes of taking a photograph?
A. Yes.
Q. Of seized items?
A. Yes. I believe downstairs there was another article of purple clothing that I photographed.
Q. Showing you Government's 29. What is 29?
A. More purple clothing in a bag.
Q. Okay. Where is that in relation to the bedroom?
A. That would be downstairs, right inside the front as soon as you came into the house.
GP: At this time, Your Honor, the Government moves for the admission of 26, 27, 28, and 29.
THE COURT: Be admitted.
(Government's Exhibit Numbers 26, 27, 28, and 29 admitted into evidence.)
DIRECT EXAMINATION BY GP (CONTINUED):
Q. Now, were the items recovered—items of clothing recovered from the bedroom in which the photographs were taken?
A. Yes.
Q. Showing you first Government's 42. Do you recognize what that is?
A. Yes. It's a purple shirt.

Q. Okay. And was it recovered from the bedroom in which the photographs were taken?
A. Yes.
Q. Government's 41. Same question.
A. Yes, sir.
Q. Government's 43?
A. Yes, sir.
MM: Objection to the Ravens insignia, Your Honor.
The Court: A legal objection or a personal objection?
MM: Just unfair.
Direct examination by GP (continued):
Q. Government's 39?
A. Yes, sir.
Q. Government's 40?
A. Yes, sir.
Q. Government's 38?
A. Yes, sir.
Q. Government's 37?
A. Yes, sir.
Q. And, finally, Government's 36?
A. Yes, sir.
Q. And for the record, what is Government's 36?
A. It's a pair of purple shorts.
GP: At this time, I move for the admission of 36, 37. And for the record, 37 is a tee shirt—an embroidered tee shirt; 38 is a striped hoodie, purple sweater; 40, a purple tee shirt with the insignia K original on the front; 39, a short-sleeved front button-up purple shirt with a photograph reading "Rest in Peace D.D."; a Ravens' long-sleeved purple tee shirt; 43; and then 41 is a gray-and-purple long-sleeved sweater. Court's indulgence.
The Court: Here's one up here.
GP: Yes. And, finally, 42 is a black-and-purple long-sleeved striped sweater. Court's indulgence. Thank you, Officer. I have no further questions, Your Honor.
Cross-examination by MM:
Q. Hello, Officer.

A. Hello, sir.
Q. Officer, you responded to 1362 Valley because who called you?
A. We were assisting the Seventh District Detective's Office with the execution of the warrant.
Q. All right. And was that Officer Hollins who called you?
A. He is one of the detectives, yes.
Q. Okay. So you were executing a—if you know, you were executing a search warrant that was related to this case, correct?
A. Yes.
Q. Not some other unrelated matter?
A. Yes.
Q. Okay. And you said you seized these purple shorts, correct?
A. Yes, they were seized.
Q. Well, they were seized. You didn't actually take them yourself?
A. I was not the seizing officer—no.
Q. Okay. And this is Government's 36. Was Officer Savoy there when you got there?
A. I don't remember.
Q. Were there any other officers there?
A. There was, you know, my unit—as far as actual people, officers on the scene that day—that would be on the warrant of who was actually in the house.
Q. Okay. But there were other officers?
A. Yes.
Q. You don't remember whether Officer Savoy was there? So—and you—you observed a number of the purple clothes, isn't that right?
A. Yes.
Q. And how many search warrants have you executed in the District of Columbia?
A. I've taken part in, let's say, an estimation of approximately a hundred.
Q. And you've seen purple clothing before, I take it?
A. I have.

Q. And purple clothing is not so unusual that you can identify an individual in the city as apart from someone else—isn't that right?
A. I guess that would depend on the circumstances.
Q. Can you see GP's tie from here?
A. I can.
Q. What color is it?
A. Purple.
Q. All right. Thank you, Officer.
REDIRECT EXAMINATION BY GP:
Q. Do you see me wearing purple shorts at the time?
A. No, I do not.
THE COURT: Thank you, Officer. You may step down.
(Witness excused.)
GP: Government calls Detective Timothy Francis.
(Therefore, TIMOTHY FRANCIS, having been called as a witness on behalf of the Government and having been first duly sworn by the deputy clerk, was examined and testified.)
DIRECT EXAMINATION BY GP:
Q. Officer Francis, good afternoon.
A. Good afternoon.
Q. How are you, sir?
A. Great.
Q. Detective Francis, introduce yourself to the ladies and gentlemen of the jury by stating and spelling your name.
A. Detective Timothy Francis, my last name is Francis, F-r-a-n-c-i-s.
Q. Detective Francis, you work for the Metropolitan Police Department, correct?
A. Yes, I do.
Q. And how long have you been there?
A. Almost twelve years.
Q. And what do you currently do?
A. I'm a detective.
Q. Are you assigned to any particular district?
A. The Seventh District.

Q. All right. Detective Francis, did you have an opportunity to determine whether or not an individual by the name of HP had a license to carry a pistol as of April 27, 2011?

A. I did.

Q. And did you also have an opportunity to ascertain whether the same HP—and by the way, that is date of birth February 26, 1986—whether he had a firearm registration certificate as of April 27, 2011?

A. I did.

Q. And what was your determination as to whether HP had a license to carry a pistol on that given day?

A. He did not.

Q. And what about HP's status as a legitimate holder of a firearm certificate on that particular day?

A. He was not.

Q. Showing you Government's 32 and 33. Take a look at those for me, Detective. Tell me if you recognize what they are.

(Witness reviews document.)

A. Yes. These are the certifications that state he does not have a license to carry a pistol or a registration in the District.

Q. As of what day?

(Witness reviews document.)

The Court: Can you direct him?

The Witness: It's dated August 19, 2011.

Direct examination by GP (continued):

Q. Okay. And what about the firearm certificate?

A. February 27, 2011.

GP: This time I move for the admission of Government's 32 and 33.

The Court: Be admitted.

(Government's Exhibit Numbers 32 and 33 admitted into evidence.)

GP: I have no further questions.

MM: No questions, Your Honor.

The Court: Thank you, Detective. You may step down.

GP: The Government rests, Your Honor.

The Court: Ladies and gentlemen, the Government has rested its evidence in this case. May I see Counsel at the bench?

(Bench conference.)

MM: Your Honor, the defense would make its motion for judgment of acquittal regarding the charges of burglary while armed, assault with a dangerous weapon, felony possession, carrying a pistol without a license, and UFUA charges. The defense argues that there was insufficient evidence, and given the standard at this stage, we submit on the record.

The Court: Okay. Just for the record, taking the evidence in the light most favorable to the Government, I'll deny it.

MM: Instruction.

The Court: Hold on a second. The felony possession is concluded; it's premature.

MM: I also left out the destruction of property charge, Your Honor.

The Court: Is there a destruction of property charge? I didn't have that in my instructions. Okay.

MM: I'm sorry. It's there. However, although there was some evidence as to the front door being kicked in, and I believe insufficient evidence that there was a bullet damage, there was no evidence whatsoever of the value of the damage.

GP: And that's why it's a misdemeanor charge, Your Honor.

MM: I thought it was a felony.

GP: No.

MM: I would love that one and just argue insufficient evidence and submit on the record.

The Court: Okay. I'll deny it for the same reasons. Tell me what you want to try to get accomplished in the next twenty minutes or so before the luncheon recess.

MM: I'd like to accomplish, by stipulation, playing some recordings of the Murray suspect, Your Honor.

The Court: So we're technically set up for that now?

MM: I am. I'm going to use the old-fashioned method—bend the mic toward my computer system—and I believe that's all I could accomplish effectively before lunch.

The Court: Okay. Have you previewed—

GP: Yes, I have.

MM: It won't take long. It will probably be about six or seven minutes.

THE COURT: And then do you have any witnesses you want to call?

MM: I do have some witnesses, Your Honor. I was going to call Detective Hollins, but I imagine he'd be fairly lengthy.

THE COURT: We can get him started. I'd like to try to get as much on as we can.

MM: I can probably get him started.

THE COURT: Okay. Thank you.

(Open court.)

THE COURT: Ladies and gentlemen, as I indicated to you at the beginning of the trial, HP is presumed to be innocent, and he's not required to produce any evidence. The defense does have the option of presenting evidence, if they wish to. So at this time I'll ask MM, Does the defense wish to present any evidence?

MM: Yes, Your Honor. The defense does.

May I have a moment, Your Honor?

The defense intends to play excerpts of an interview and would read into the record the following stipulation.

THE COURT: First of all, ladies and gentlemen, a stipulation is an agreement between the parties as to facts. Rather than calling witnesses to Court to testify about matters that are not in dispute, the parties can reach an agreement that saves a lot of trial time, so you may accept these facts to be true.

MM: The parties stipulate and agree that the following three audio clips, identified as Defense Exhibit 3A, 3B, and 3C, are excerpts from an interview of MB, which was conducted on June 8, 2011, by a representative of the Child Advocacy Center. And, Your Honor, I have prepared transcripts, which I've shown to Counsel, and I believe he does not object to them.

THE COURT: Okay. Ladies and gentlemen, again, the transcripts are not evidence. They're merely documents to assist you in listening to the tapes. To the extent there's a conflict between the transcript and/or the tapes, your memory and conclusion as to what's on the tapes should prevail.

MM: May I hand them out? May I? I'm going to ask everybody to just pass these out. Take one. They're marked 1, 2, and 3 at the top of the page. I'll wait until everyone has a copy, Your Honor, and then I'll begin.

The defense will be playing 3A.

(Playing tape.)

MM: For the record, the defense will be playing what's been identified as Defense Exhibit 3A, which is Cut 2 on the transcript.

(Playing tape.)

MM: For the record, the defense will now be playing what's been marked for identification as Defense Exhibit 3A, listed as Cut 2 on the transcript.

(Playing tape.)

MM: For the record, the defense will now be playing what is marked for identification as Defense Exhibit 3A, marked on the transcripts as Cut 3A—excuse me—Defense Exhibit 3C, marked on the transcripts as 3A.

(Playing tape.)

MM: And that concludes the audio portion of it. I will collect the transcript.

Excuse me, Your Honor. May I approach with Counsel?

The Court: Uh-huh.

(Bench conference.)

MM: It's probably nothing, Your Honor, but the young woman in the front row, second from the right, in a sort of cream-colored shirt, was trying to answer your question. I did not respond, so I asked to approach.

The Court: Okay. Thank you.

MM: Very well.

(Open court.)

The Court: Do you have a question? You have to—

The Juror: I have to go to the bathroom.

The Court: Okay. That's great. We're going to take a luncheon recess now. 2:15. 2:15. Do not discuss the case among yourselves or with anyone. Thank you.

(Jurors out at 12:50 p.m.)

The Court: Let me just go over a couple of things on the instructions now that we have time.

Do you mind, frankly, if I excuse the court reporter for lunch and you summarize any instructions after lunch?

MM: I don't object, Your Honor. The blue man's on.

GP: I don't object, Your Honor.

THE COURT: Thank you.

(Off the record.)

THE COURT: I was going to do a Boyd inquiry now, MM. Do you want me to do it now or—

MM: Yes, Your Honor.

THE COURT: HP, we're now in the defense case, and during the defense case, you'll have the right to testify or not testify. Whether or not you testify, it's your decision and your decision alone.

Obviously, consider the advice of MM, but you make the personal decision about whether you wish to testify.

If you wish to testify, you'd be placed under oath, asked questions by your lawyer, and cross-examined by the Government. If you do not wish to testify, I'll instruct the jury not to consider your decision in any way in determining whether the Government has proved the case beyond a reasonable doubt.

Do you understand your right to testify?

THE DEFENDANT: Yes, Your Honor.

THE COURT: MM, do—I was going to go through all the questions now, or do you want me to wait until a later time?

MM: I believe HP is electing not to testify, Your Honor, and I doubt very seriously that will change. If it's going to be at the end, that's fine.

MM: I don't think that—I don't think that the evidence is going to change or impact this argument.

THE COURT: Okay. I didn't know that. Okay. I'll hear you then.

MM: And they're tied together, obviously. The self-defense and the flight—without the self-defense, obviously, there's no argument for the flight. The flight goes to self-defense. So they either both go up or they both fall, and I would suggest to the Court that or enlighten the Court to the standard, which is exceedingly low when it comes to self-defense instruction.

THE COURT: I agree with that.

MM: Any evidence that tends to show, and the jury is, of course, free to discredit some or all of the Government's witnesses. Indeed, it would be possible in this case, given the flight, given the inconsistencies in the testimony, and given witness JH's statements that were introduced to the jury, that HP did not shoot—shoot at him. On various occasions, JH said that. They've been apprised of that. It would be possible for them to conclude that it was JH who was doing the shooting or that JH had a gun and threatened HP with it, such that HP shot back in self-defense, as evidenced by JH's immediate flight and then hiding from police.

It's not the strongest argument in the world, and quite frankly, I don't know if I'm going to make it during my closing.

THE COURT: I didn't hear that. I heard your opening. I was sort of surprised at the request since the opening seemed to focus on something else.

MM: It did, and I don't know that I'm going to make that argument because, obviously, it's not the strongest argument the defense has in this case. But it is an argument, and I believe it's sufficient to give rise to the need for an instruction, whether the defense argues it or not.

THE COURT: So, but doesn't that argument—and I'll hear from GP—come down to—obviously I'm simplifying it, but if a complaining witness in an ADW case initially denied that a particular person did the ADW and then accuses that person of ADW, somehow that gets converted into—you don't have to believe them on the ADW, and in addition, you can affirmatively believe that he's the one—the complaining witness is the one who did the ADW.

MM: Even though I view the standard as exceedingly small, I would not argue that in—under that scenario, we would be entitled to instruction. I believe it's the design coupled with the immediate flight and the—

THE COURT: And was the flight—just from your point of view, is the Court to conclude from his testimony that the flight was from HP allegedly or from the police?

MM: I plan on arguing he's hiding from the police, Your Honor. He certainly remained hiding long after whoever was shooting in the house had gone until the police found him some thirty minutes later.

The Court: Right. I was asking about the flight, though, not the hiding.

I thought the—as I remember the testimony—GP, I'll hear from you—I thought it was allegedly a flight from the assailants as opposed to the police.

MM: I don't think JH actually said he was running forth. I think the most logical insinuation would be that he was running from whoever was shooting if, in fact, he was shooting at him or—or even if they were both shooting at each other or threatening each other with guns.

The Court: Okay.

MM: So I don't think that impacts the argument. I'm left with—I'm left with denials that it was HP shooting at him and immediate flight and hiding from the police, which is not the strongest argument in the world, but sufficient for the instruction.

The Court: Thank you.

GP: Your Honor, the Government would argue that there is absolutely insufficient basis for either instruction of self-defense or flight. The defendant lost his right to argue self-defense when he became the aggressor and burst into the house with a firearm and then discharged the firearm. There's no evidence—

The Court: I think his theory is that, to the extent there's evidence, he may have burst into the house, but there—he was unarmed, and it was—as I understand what MM is saying—

GP: And I understand that, Your Honor, but again, there was simply no evidence to support that HP was indeed unarmed. We've got no evidence to suggest that he was. Also, any inconsistencies, any original denials, or any attempt to cower from JH or anyone else—as the Court has pointed out—does not necessarily flip this into a situation in which HP is suddenly the victim. All the evidence—all the evidence suggests in this case, in terms of flight, is that JH was, number one, afraid for his life. You heard testimony that he jumped off the balcony in an attempt to get away from the scene of the shooting, and he also was afraid of bringing any undue attention to the house that his friend owned, and that was one of the reasons he articulated for not coming forth originally.

THE COURT: GP, can you refresh my memory? Was JH's initial statements, were they denials that the ADW occurred, or were they a failure to accuse somebody of the ADW that did occur?

GP: His—his only statement throughout these proceedings—the Court heard the very first 911 call, which was just a few minutes after the event. There were two 911 calls in which he specifically identified HP.

THE COURT: Right. But has he—has he ever denied—

GP: He has—he has never denied that, Your Honor.

THE COURT: The ADW?

GP: The ADW. In terms of his grand jury presentation, he has never denied it before me. The only indication that I've ever gotten that perhaps there was a change in his story was when I had a conversation with MM about a conversation he had with JH in the jail, maybe a day or two before we began the trial—that was the only indication.

THE COURT: Right. Okay. So at least initially, he's—he didn't deny the ADW, he just did not accuse HP initially of the ADW.

GP: When is—how does the Court define *initial*?

THE COURT: Prior to his conversation with MM.

MM: The testimony, Your Honor, was that the officer said, "Why is your cousin shooting at you?" And he said, "My cousin's not."

THE COURT: Right. But that's—

GP: But that wasn't the initial—

THE COURT: Right. But I guess—I understand.

I'm just trying to clarify there's a difference between denying the ADW and then claiming that an ADW occurred and then either accusing or not accusing. There's a difference in my mind.

At this point, for the purposes of preparing your closing arguments, I'm not inclined to give a self-defense instruction, but I—GP, I ask you to run it by the Appellate Division in your office to make sure the Court's on correct footing, and then I think MM is correct that the standard is so low that the—I have at least minimal concern that it may have been triggered, but at this point, I am not inclined to give the self-defense instruction.

MM: Will be denied with the flight instruction, correct, Your Honor?

THE COURT: Correct. Let me just ask you, is it easier for you for me to print out hard copies of the draft as to where we stand now, or do you want me to send them electronically?

MM: Easier for me electronically.

GP: That's fine.

THE COURT: Okay. I'm going to send that now.

And can I ask you, MM, you obviously—you don't have to preview, but just in terms of the afternoon, is it likely we'll be arguing, or what's your guess on that?

MM: You know, I think it's fifty-fifty—we will be arguing. We're coming back at 2:15; 3:00—it'll be close. But if I had to bet my money, I'd bet we would be arguing.

THE COURT: Okay. I just wanted both sides to be prepared.

GP: Does the Court instruct first?

THE COURT: I instruct up until the section that's entitled "Deliberations."

GP: Okay.

THE COURT: And then I—I would just say if that's your plan, we may have to manage the time—people have to argue, so—

MM: I think we'll be arguing.

THE COURT: Okay.

MM: And I can tell you I have Detective Collins—Hollins, who I intend to call. GP tells me that Officer Pulaski is available. I did not subpoena Officer Pulaski, but I asked GP if he would make her available to me.

GP: That's the only reason she's here.

MM: Appreciate all that, Your Honor. GP has been gracious throughout this entire litigation, and I may have a short civilian witness.

THE COURT: Okay. So we might be able to conclude by 3:00?

MM: Yeah.

THE COURT: Well, take a look at the instructions, and then we'll—if you have any other suggestions, let me know. Thank you to the court reporter. And I agree GP has been very professional in this case.

GP: Thank you, Your Honor.

(Luncheon recess taken at 1:30 p.m.)

Afternoon Session

THE COURT: Ready for the jury.

THE DEPUTY CLERK: Calling for the record *United States v. HP*, 2011 CF3-8205.

MM: MM for HP, who's present, Your Honor.

GP: Good afternoon, Your Honor. GP for the United States.

THE COURT: Why don't you have your next witness.

MM: Very well, Your Honor.

Should the officer take the stand, Your Honor?

THE COURT: Good afternoon.

THE WITNESS: Hello.

THE COURT: You can be seated.

(Jury in at 2:29 p.m.)

THE DEPUTY CLERK: Could you please stand and raise your right hand for me, ma'am? Thank you.

(Therefore, CHELSEA PULASKI, having been called as a witness on behalf of the Government and having been first duly sworn by the deputy clerk, was examined and testified.)

DIRECT EXAMINATION BY MM:

Q. Good afternoon, Officer.

A. Hello.

Q. Could you please state your first name, your last name, and spell your first and last name for the court reporter?

A. Okay. My name is Officer Chelsea Pulaski. First name C-h-e-l-s-e-a; last name Pulaski, P-u-l-a-s-k-i.

Q. And, Ms. Pulaski, where are you employed?

A. Metropolitan Police Department, Seventh District.

Q. And you're an officer, correct?

A. Yes, I am.
Q. And how long have you been an officer?
A. Three years next month.
Q. And what's your assigned duty?
A. I am a crime patrol unit on daywork.
Q. You're a what?
A. Crime patrol.
Q. Oh, crime patrol.
A. It was originally burglary suppression.
Q. And back in April of 2011, were you working with a partner, or were you working by yourself?
A. I was with my partner.
Q. And who was your partner?
A. Officer Smith.
Q. Okay. And on that exact date, April 27, 2011, did you have occasion to be called to 1435 Good Hope Road?
A. Yes, I did.
Q. And that was in response to a radio run?
A. Yes, it was.
Q. And when you first got there—well, first let me ask you, that's a single house that's sandwiched between a school and a barbershop, correct?
A. Yes, that's correct.
Q. And there's a stone wall in front of the house with a lawn that leads up to the porch of the residence, correct?
A. Correct. The steps lead up to the porch.
Q. Okay. When you first got there on the call, before going inside, are you able to estimate for our jury about how many people were out there in front of the house?
A. No, I don't remember.
Q. Okay. What about in front of the barbershop?
A. No, I don't remember. I didn't look at the barbershop.
Q. Did you have an opportunity to speak with the woman who identified herself as MB?
A. Yes.
Q. Okay. And when you first pulled up, where was she?

A. I believe she was in the house. Officer Smith and I pulled up, and then Officer Majuhid—he was working by himself—so the two scout cars, we pulled up at the same time. Officer Majuhid and I approached the house by ourselves, and Officer Smith went back into the scout car to go canvass. We walked up the steps and went to the house, and I believe MB was at the front door.

Q. Okay. And so you were the first officers that you could see who responded to the radio run, correct?

A. Yes. It didn't take us that long to get there.

Q. Okay. And you did have an opportunity to speak with MB about what happened, correct?

A. Yes.

Q. Okay. And do you know a Detective Hollins?

A. Yes.

Q. Okay. And did you have an opportunity to speak with MB before Detective Hollins arrived?

A. Yes.

Q. MB told you that someone had shot in the house, correct?

A. Yes.

Q. She was unable to identify to you before Detective Hollins got there—she was unable to identify to you who that person was, correct?

A. From the moment we got there, she was very upset, almost hysterical. And we asked her what happened, and she said that they were shooting. They shot in the house; they were shooting the house. So we said, "Are they still in there?" And she said, "No." But we needed to make sure that they still weren't in there.

At that point, we said we needed everybody out of the house, onto the front porch, and that's when Officer Majuhid and I went into the house to make sure that the shooters weren't still in there.

Q. All right. After you did that—

A. Yes.

Q. Did you have another—

A. Yes.

Q. After you did that, did you have another opportunity to speak with MB before Detective Hollins arrived?
A. Yes, I did. I spoke to a bunch of people who were standing in that front parlor area. There were about five or six people.
Q. Let me ask you about that. When you say front parlor area, do you mean inside the house?
A. Yes, inside the house.
Q. Okay. So in addition to MB, there were how many people in the house?
A. I can't tell you exactly, but I know that on seeing all of the people who were in the house at the time, we had to make sure they were detained at the house so they couldn't leave. There were two people in the basement, there was a son in the bed, there was a son with the mom.
Q. And you don't remember about how many people there were or their names?
A. I wrote some in my notebook, but I can't tell you off the top of my head, no.
Q. Would reviewing your notes refresh recollection?
A. Sure.
Q. I'm going to show you what's been marked for identification only as Defense Exhibit 4. Take as much time as you need, Officer.
A. Okay.
Q. Well, first, take a look at that and then tell when you're done.
A. Okay. Yeah. The bottom here looks like I have four people: MB, EB, KW, JR. Those are my notes, yes.
Q. Okay. Now take as much time as you need to review your notes and just look up the jury. Those are your notes, correct?
A. Yes.
Q. And those would have been the people that you just described interviewing or speaking to in the parlor area?
A. I mean I can't say for certain, but I know that I got their names when I was on scene. It's all chronological here, so that would have been later. I didn't sit and write their names. I was obviously trying to get the suspect, understand what happened, and figure out what was going on.

Q. Sure. But based on your notes, those people were in the house, at least when you got there, correct?
A. Yes.
Q. Okay. And you say you don't remember how many people were outside?
A. No, not when we walked—when we got there. I believe the call was for shooting in the house, and so I know that Officer Majuhid and I—our first instinct was to go into the house, and I don't really remember who was out front of the barbershop or anything like that.
Q. All right. Now, I understand you don't remember how many people were out there.
A. Right.
Q. But if you don't remember the answer to this question, just go ahead and tell me you don't remember.
A. Okay.
Q. Do you remember whether there were any people out there on Good Hope Road?
A. I honestly don't. I can't say.
Q. Okay. Now, after you secured the house to make sure there was nobody else in the house—
A. Yes.
Q. —there was no one with a weapon in the house, correct? That's what you were looking for, right?
A. Correct, of course.
Q. For the safety of everyone?
A. And the victims.
Q. And you had an opportunity to speak with MB again, correct?
A. Yes. After we came down the stairs, I was speaking to her, trying to get from the people there what happened and a better suspect lookout than what we had been given over the radio, so the units out in the field could canvass more effectively.
Q. Okay. And I just want to be careful about the time period I'm asking about. What I'm asking you now is the time period before Detective Hollins arrived.
A. Right. He's still not there at this point.

Q. Okay.
A. We went upstairs, looked around the rooms, came back down. It's probably been a couple of minutes at this point.
Q. Okay. And during that period of time, after you—by that I mean after you, you know, canvassed the house for everybody's safety—
A. Yes.
Q. —but before Detective Hollins arrived—while you were speaking with MB, during that period of time, she never mentioned the name HP to you, correct?
A. No, she did not.
Q. She never told you that JH or JH's cousin was the one who had shot up the house, correct?
A. I'm sorry?
Q. She never said to you, before Detective Hollins arrived, that it was JH's cousin who had shot up the house?
A. No.
Q. In fact, she never told you that the person who had shot up the house had been there earlier with a gun threatening JH, correct?
A. No, she did not. She was very reluctant to talk to me.
Q. Now, did you have the opportunity to meet MB?
A. He was standing there when I was—I'm trying to create a picture just based on what I remember. We came back down the stairs and had them come into that front foyer; the children were there, the mother was there.
Q. I don't mean to cut you off, but I do want to ask you a very specific question. It simply is, Did you have an opportunity to speak with the person named MB?
A. Okay. I did, and everyone was there at the time.
Q. Okay. And he's a little kid?
A. Yes, a little kid.
Q. About nine years old?
A. Uh-huh.
Q. Okay. And this, again, is before Detective Hollins arrived, correct?
A. Yes.

Q. Okay. And while you were speaking with MB, did he ever tell you that he personally came downstairs and observed the shooters get into a black truck and drive off?
A. It's—no, when you asked specifically like that.
Q. I am kind of asking specifically like that.
A. Okay.
Q. And during the period of time when you first got there—
A. Yes.
Q. —when you first went in the house, was MB the first person you saw?
A. I believe so.
Q. Okay. Was MB there?
A. There were a bunch of kids that ran out. I would imagine he would have been. He wasn't my focus.
Q. To be fair, you don't know for sure?
A. Yeah.
Q. All right. And when you went to search the house, do you know if MB was with his mom?
A. I don't know.
Q. Okay. How long did it take you to search the house?
A. Just a couple of minutes, maybe. Maybe a minute, at most. We were just doing a very visual search for victims and the shooter. We noticed what appeared to be bullet holes going up to the attic.
Q. But you weren't doing a crime scene search?
A. No.
Q. Okay. You were, as you said, searching for victims?
A. Victims.
Q. Making sure the place was safe, correct?
A. Yes.
Q. Okay. And you're not trained as a crime scene technician, correct?
A. No.
Q. Okay. Because you said bullet holes, right?
A. Yes.
Q. Okay. And so I have to ask you. You didn't look behind the wall to see if there were any bullets in there, right?

A. No. I'm not formally trained in any firearms to that extent.
Q. Okay. And while you were—who was conducting this, you know, this cursory search? Just to make sure everything was safe, who was conducting that?
A. Myself and Officer Majuhid.
Q. Okay. What about Officer Smith?
A. He was back in the scout car, and he went to go canvass to see who was out still, with all the other officers.
Q. I take it as far as you know then there were no officers remaining with the witnesses while you conducted the search?
A. I'm not sure who showed up after us. No, I don't know.
MM: May I have the Court's indulgence for a moment, Your Honor? I'm about to finish.
(Pause.)
MM: Well, thank you, Officer Pulaski.
CROSS-EXAMINATION BY GP:
Q. Good afternoon, Officer Pulaski.
A. Hello.
Q. Can you characterize for us the demeanor of MB as you were discussing these events with her?
A. She appeared very upset, traumatized. She seemed legitimately frightened, and I think because of that, we had the urgency to get everybody out. It just seemed like there was a real trauma that had just occurred.
Q. Did you take her out of the house to talk to her one-on-one?
A. No, I did not.
Q. Did you take her down to the Seventh District, where it was quiet to talk to her one-on-one?
A. No, I did not.
Q. How long was the conversation that you had between yourself and MB?
A. Maybe a total from the—the first time I saw her or when I had come down the stairs and spoke to her between myself and MB? Briefly, total?
Q. Let's talk about each individual conversation. How long was the first?

A. The first, just a couple of statements, just to get the gist, madc sure no one was injured, or either "If everyone is okay, stay out here." And then the second one maybe maximum a minute when I was trying to get additional information on the suspect.
Q. And you—you were shown some notes by MM, correct?
A. Yes.
Q. And this has been marked as Defense Number 4. Take a look at these notes for me and tell me if there's any indication of what MB told you during the course of those two conversations you had with her.
MM: Objection, Your Honor, outside scope.
The Court: Overrule.
The Witness: I'm not really sure. Oh, down here. I opened the door, all I saw was a black gun. I believe that was MB.
Cross-examination by GP (continued):
Q. And if MB had told you or given you any further details, you would have written those details in those notes, correct?
A. Yes.
Q. Okay.
A. Yes. Probably. I write down a lot of things.
Q. And you're a good officer, correct? You take good notes, don't you?
A. I take good notes, yes.
Q. Did you get an impression as to the willingness of MB to even talk to you?
MM: Objection, Your Honor, calls for speculation.
The Court: I'll overrule.
The Witness: I had a dealing with MB before, and she—
MM: Objection.
The Court: Sustained as to that.
The Witness: Okay.
Cross-examination by GP (continued):
Q. —— that you're looking at Defense Number 4, of any additional information that you gained from MB, correct?
A. No. I tried to be chronological in all of my notes, but sometimes I write around different—I write things on the side or on the bottom, but it—

The Court: Only this incident.

The Witness: Okay. She just was very reluctant to want to talk to me. She was a bit, a bit hesitant, frightened, didn't want to give a lot of details at the time to me.

Cross-examination by GP (continued):

Q. Okay. It was also mentioned by defense counsel, Officer, regarding MB?

A. Yes.

Q. And did you had a conversation with MB as well, correct?

A. I did. I was speaking with his mother, and the people that were there were chiming in about what had happened and the vehicle and the lookout, and that's when I overheard MB make the comment.

MM: Objection, Your Honor.

The Court: Sustained as to that.

Cross-examination by GP (continued):

Q. You had a conversation with MB in the company of other individuals, is that what you're testifying to?

A. Yes.

Q. Did you have an opportunity to take MB down to the Seventh District?

A. No, I do not.

Q. Did you have a chance to talk to MB in private at any time?

A. No, I did not.

Q. How long did you talk to MB?

A. A couple of statements back and forth, not long.

Q. I have nothing further. Thank you, Officer.

Redirect examination by MM:

Q. So when you were—you said when you were talking to MB, other people were chiming in, correct?

A. Well, they were—the family was standing in the foray while I was talking to the mother. They were talking about the black car and the spinners and the—

Q. I'm going to stop you for a second. Let me ask you. While you were talking with MB, were other people chiming in as you just described it?

A. No. When I spoke to him and what I heard him say, I heard him—I overheard him say, "I know who did it," and I was like—
Q. Let me ask you.
A. —and then I spoke just to him.
GP: Objection. If she can answer the question.
THE COURT: Overruled.
REDIRECT EXAMINATION BY MM (CONTINUED):
Q. When MB said that, "I know who did it"—
A. Uh-huh.
Q. —to other people around, correct, from the family members? Correct?
A. There were.
Q. And correct me if I'm wrong, but you testified that they were all chiming in at the same time trying to tell you—if I may finish.
A. Okay.
Q. —at the same time trying to tell you what happened, correct?
A. Before he made that statement, yes.
Q. Okay. And it was after that that he made that statement, correct?
A. It was during the chaos of trying to get the suspect information, the lookout, yes, that he made that statement, and I picked up on it. I heard—I heard the little voice, and I drew my attention to him.
Q. Let me ask you a different question.
A. Okay.
Q. —— all I saw was a black gun. Is that right?
A. I read that from my notes, and I believe that's—
Q. You testified that MB told you, "I opened the door, and all I saw was a black gun." Is that right?
A. —— what she said. I wrote it down. I don't have it in quotes, and I don't have her name next to it, but I believe that's what she told me.
Q. Okay. And not to nitpick, but the reason you believe that's what she told you is because you wrote it in your notes, correct?
A. I wrote it in my notes, and I remember her saying something very similar to that.

Q. Okay. So, in other words, she didn't say, "I opened the door, and I saw a person and described him." She said, "I opened the door, and all I saw was a black gun."
A. If that's what I wrote, that's what she said.
Q. Okay. Well, thank you again, Officer.
A. Okay.
GP: Follow up with one question, Your Honor?
The Court: One.
Recross-examination by GP:
Q. When was the first time you heard the name HP mentioned?
MM: Objection, Your Honor. May we approach?
The Court: Uh-huh.
(Bench conference.)
The Court: Do you have a proffer as to what the answer is going to be?
GP: From MB?
MM: This officer knows HP.
The Court: Excuse me?
MM: I believe this officer knows HP.
GP: That's not the basis upon which I'm asking the question.
The Court: That's not what the question was.
MM: Just like the question was—was open-ended enough: "When was the first time you heard the name HP?"
The Court: He's exactly right.
GP: I'm sorry. He's exactly right.
The Court: Correct.
GP: On that day—that's right.
The Court: In—on that day, in that foyer?
GP: That's right. I stand corrected.
The Court: Thank you.
(Open court.)
The Court: You may resume the stand. Thank you.
Recross-examination by GP (continued):
Q. Now, Officer, in connection with the investigation of this case on April 27, 2011, inside the foyer area of 1435 Good Hope Road, when was the very first time—and who did you—strike

that. When was the very first time you heard the word HP mentioned as a possible suspect?

A. The first time I heard the name HP was by MB.

Q. Thank you.

MM: Do I get one, too, Your Honor?

The Court: You do.

Redirect examination by MM:

Q. And when MB said this name, HP, this was after the period of time when other people were around and chiming in and trying to explain what happened, correct?

A. Yes.

Q. Thank you.

The Court: Thank you. You may step down. Next witness, please.

(Witness excused.)

MM: Yes, Your Honor. The defense calls Detective Hollins.

(Therefore, Rodney Hollins, having been called as a witness on behalf of the Government and having been first duly sworn by the deputy clerk, was examined and testified.)

Direct examination by MM:

Q. Hello, Detective.

A. Good evening.

Q. Detective, you know the drill for our court reporter. Could you state your first name and your last name and spell both of them, please?

A. First name is Rodney, R-o-d-n-e-y, Hollins, H-o-l-l-i-n-s.

Q. And you're employed by the MPD, correct?

A. Yes.

Q. And what's your rank?

A. Detective.

Q. And how long have you been a detective?

A. Seventeen years.

Q. And how long have you been with MPD?

A. Twenty.

Q. I want to draw your attention to April 27, 2011. You had the occasion to go to 1435 Good Hope Road that day, correct?

A. Yes.

Q. And you were there responding to a possible burglary, correct?
A. Yes.
Q. And do you know how long after the first radio run was—was issued that you arrived? In other words, do you know how much time elapsed between the time from the first radio run and to the time you would have arrived?
A. Approximately five to ten minutes. It's not that far from the Seventh District, that location.
Q. Five to—I'm sorry. Five to ten minutes.
A. Five to ten minutes.
Q. When you arrived there, there were already uniformed officers on the scene, correct?
A. Yes.
Q. And you had an opportunity to speak with some witnesses in connection with this alleged burglary, correct?
A. Yes.
Q. And one of the witnesses you spoke with was MB, isn't that right?
A. Yes.
Q. Who identified herself as the leaseholder of the property, correct?
A. Yes.
Q. And MB described someone breaking into her house and shooting inside the house, correct?
A. Yes.
Q. And one of the things that she told you was that the person that broke in with the gun actually pointed the gun in her face, correct?
GP: Objection, leading.
The Court: Overruled.
The Witness: No.
Direct examination by MM (continued):
Q. You completed the affidavit for a search warrant in this case, correct, Detective?
A. Yes.
Q. And I'm going to show you what's been marked for identification as Defense Exhibit Number 5. I'm going to hand this to you

and ask you a simple question. First, that's your affidavit that you completed for a search warrant, correct?
A. Yes.
Q. In connection with this particular case, correct?
A. Yes.
Q. Okay. I'm going to draw your attention so I can cut the time, and if you'd lay it down on the table, I would be able to do it faster.
The paragraph 3 isn't it true in your affidavit you wrote in paragraph 3 for Counsel, second sentence: "MB reports the defendant pointed a black handgun in her face."
A. Yes.
Q. All right. And that was an affidavit that you swore to in order to get a search warrant, correct?
A. Yes.
Q. Okay. Was she also—initially indicated that she did not know who the gunman was, correct, when you first spoke to her? Isn't that correct?
A. Yes.
Q. Okay. And you had asked her for a description. The description she gave you was very vague, correct?
A. Yes.
Q. And initially she gave you no description of the other person that was with this gunman, correct?
A. Yes.
Q. She told you that the door had been kicked in, correct?
A. Yes.
Q. All right. And that she had not even gotten to the door when it had been kicked in, correct?
A. Yes.
Q. In other words, she did not tell you that she got to the door, looked out a window, and saw who was outside, correct?
GP: Your Honor, I object to the leading.
THE COURT: It's a little leading. You got to modify your question a little.
MM: Very well, Your Honor. I will.
DIRECT EXAMINATION BY MM (CONTINUED):

Q. Now, initially—well, I should say at some point during your interview of MB, she mentioned the name HP, correct?
A. Yes.
Q. Okay. But prior to that—prior to that, she did not identify who the gunman was. For example, she didn't say it was JH's cousin?
A. No.
Q. Did she say anything to you about this gunman coming to that location prior, on a prior occasion that same day?
A. Not that same day. She mentioned that the—
Q. I want to ask you right now, we're going to get to those other conversations later. Right now I'm going to kind of focus, I guess, my questions on what happened at the initial interview.
A. Sure.
Q. And so at that initial interview, she didn't say anything about HP coming by earlier that day, correct?
A. No.
Q. She certainly didn't say he came by with a gun, correct?
A. No.
Q. She told you she heard two shots fired during that initial interview you had with her—she told you that she had left the house and then she had heard two shots, correct?
A. Yes.
Q. Now, while you were interviewing MB, there was another witness by the name of MB being interviewed by officers, is that right?
A. Yes.
Q. About how far from where you were interviewing MB were these officers interviewing Little MB?
A. Little MB was in the next—the next room over. I interviewed MB in the foyer or in the living room.
Q. Okay. And—it was the next room over because it was like a room separator or an archway separating the living room from the dining room, correct?
A. Yes.
Q. All right. But there is no door separating those two rooms, correct?
A. No.

Q. So it's one continuous space with the exception of the archway, correct?
A. Yes.
Q. And, in fact, while you were interviewing MB—the period that I'm now asking you about is when you were interviewing MB before she mentioned the name HP—another officer came over and had a conversation with you, correct?
A. Yes.
Q. All right. And which officer was that? Was it Smith or Pulaski?
A. Pulaski.
Q. Okay. And Pulaski, from where you were standing, had been talking to Little MB, correct?
A. Yes.
Q. Okay. And she came over to you and pulled you to the side and told you that MB had said the name HP, correct?
A. Yes.
Q. And that was about, what, ten to fifteen feet from where MB was standing when Pulaski said that, correct?
A. I don't know the distance between the foyer and behind the wall. I don't know how close he was.
Q. All right. But you do remember testifying at the preliminary hearing, though, correct?
A. Yes.
Q. And you testified at the preliminary hearing on May 26, 2011. Does that date sound about right, Detective?
A. Yes.
MM: Okay. Court's indulgence for a moment. Page 45, lines 1 to 6 for Counsel.
Direct examination by MM (continued):
Q. My mistake. I want to ask you questions about the preliminary hearing in this case. You testified at the preliminary hearing, correct?
A. Yes.
Q. And that was on or about May 26, 2011, correct?
A. Yes.

Q. All right. And you were under oath at the preliminary hearing, just like you're under oath now, correct?
A. Yes.
Q. And I was at that preliminary hearing as well, asking you questions, correct?
A. Yes.
Q. And isn't it true that you were asked the following questions at that preliminary hearing and gave the following answers?

> Question: You said this officer pulled you to the side to tell you that witness one had said HP.
>
> And you said, uh-huh.
>
> Question: Could you just, for the record, describe how far to the side you were pulled?
>
> And your answer was: 10 to 15 feet.

Do you need to review it, Officer?
A. No, if you're reading from the transcript.
Q. Well, first of all, you were asked those questions, and you gave those answers, correct?
A. Yes.
Q. And back in May of 2011, when this preliminary hearing occurred, that was a lot closer in time to the event, April 27, than it is today, correct?
A. Yes.
Q. Is it fair to say your recollection of what happened might be slightly better in May than it is now?
A. Yes.
Q. Now, MB—after this officer—strike that. After Officer Pulaski came and told you the name HP, it was after that that MB said the name HP, correct?
A. Yes.
GP: Your Honor, may we have just a few more opening questions?
The Court: I think that's fair, MM.
MM: Sorry, Your Honor.
The Court: I know it's a little odd.

MM: Force of habit.
THE COURT: I agree.
DIRECT EXAMINATION BY MM (CONTINUED):
Q. You also had a brief opportunity on the scene to interview Little MB, correct?
A. Yes.
Q. And about how old was MB?
A. He looks to be ten to twelve—something like around that age bracket.
Q. And when you were interviewing him, was that alone or were there other people around?
A. Officer Pulaski was there, and maybe Officer Smith.
Q. What about his mom?
A. No, the mom wasn't there. I don't remember her.
Q. Okay. Where was it, if you remember, where you interviewed MB?
A. In the room adjacent to the foyer, which is the room around the corner from the foyer.
Q. What's a foyer?
A. It's the little short hallway when you first come into the house. It's where the chandeliers are in the middle, and around the corner from there is another room.
Q. Is that sort of what would normally be a living room in the home?
A. Around the corner?
Q. Yes.
A. Yes.
Q. Okay. And that's the room where you interviewed MB?
A. Yes.
Q. Is that the same room where you interviewed MB?
A. No. No.
Q. I must be mixed-up. What room did you interview MB in?
A. In the living room, the foyer—when you first come into the door. That's the foyer area. That's where I talked to her.
Q. Okay.
A. MB was in the adjacent room around the corner from there.
Q. All right. So is it fair to say that's the next room?

A. The next room.
Q. Okay. And you don't know where MB was when you spoke with MB?
A. No. I—I left speaking to her in the foyer to go meet with Officer Pulaski and MB in another room.
Q. Oh, so you went—after you were done with MB, you went directly to MB who was in the next room, is that right?
A. I wasn't done with MB. It was brought to my attention from Ms. Pulaski the information that she wanted to share with me.
Q. Okay. And did MB tell you anything about confronting two individuals in the hallway?
A. Yes.
Q. As a matter of fact, he told you that that's where you confronted the person with the gun in the hallway, right?
A. Yes.
Q. In other words, in the house, he didn't say he was simply viewing them from in his bed. He said he had actually run into them in the hallway?
A. Yes.
Q. Did he tell you—did he tell you where he saw them from? In other words, from what room in the house they came from?
A. No.
Q. In fact, he told you he didn't know from what room that he came, right?
A. I didn't ask him what room did he—he just said he saw him in the hallway when he came out his room.
Q. Page 29, preliminary hearing, 6 to 14, for Counsel. Ask you another question from your preliminary hearing that we talked about earlier.
A. Sure.
Q. Detective, isn't it true that you were asked if a gentlemen came, he just merely saw them in the hallway, correct? And your answer was yes.
A. So I have to ask you: Were you asked those preliminary questions, and you gave the following answers?

Question: So based in your interview of witness number 1, witness number 1 didn't know from where these two questions, and did you give that answer at the preliminary hearing?
A. Yes.
Q. Okay. Does that refresh your recollection about what MB might have told you about whether he knew from what room they came?
A. Yes.
Q. So did he know?
A. What room?
Q. Yeah.
A. Well, that's what I'm asking you.
Q. Oh.
A. MB couldn't tell you from what room—
Q. Oh, no.
A. No. Because he didn't know.
Q. No. No. And you had asked him?
GP: Your Honor, for purposes of refreshing recollection, we'd ask that the question be on the transcript—
The Court: I actually think they're saying the same thing, but we can move on.
MM: Just going to move on, if that's all right, Your Honor.
Direct examination by MM (continued):
Q. And when you were interviewing MB in the house at the scene there, did he give you a—give any description of a getaway vehicle for these individuals?
A. No.
Q. Now, I'm going to switch to JH. You may know him as JH. You know who I'm talking about, correct?
A. Yes.
Q. And you had an opportunity to speak with JH too?
A. Yes.
Q. Did you speak with him at the scene?
A. Yes.
Q. Okay. And JH initially said that there had been a shooting, but the shooter was not HP, correct?

A. I can't recall that statement. No.
Q. At the house, did he mention the name HP to you?
A. Yes.
Q. And he told you HP was trying to kill him because he saw HP shoot up the barbershop, correct?

AFTERWORD

This book is presented as my memoir, but truth be told, it's not entirely about me. It's more about the message it represents through my life choices, which led me through the judicial system. Going to trial redefined my future and helped me embark on a spiritual journey to realize that betterment and prosperity are inevitable for all who not only understand and respect but adhere to the laws of the land and the attraction of cause and effect.

This book is meant to serve as an inspiration, to agitate. My goal is to inspire and uplift people to do something they think they can't or want to do but are just unaware of the infinite possibilities life has to offer one who seeks to reveal them. I aim to agitate.

I want to take my readers on a journey through the entire trial and appeal process, including the release from prison, so they can learn firsthand how the judicial system is a world of its own. You will understand that you may be convicted of something you are innocent of or how you can be exonerated from a crime you're guilty of beyond a reasonable doubt, making the walls transparent and exposing the system's flaws. Moreover, this book aims to make people aware of issues that have been overlooked for too long and to pass along valuable information or help someone through trying times so they can come out on the better side of their situation.

Additionally, I now aim to be a vigorous public advocate for justice, a symbol of peace, and a recognized leader of an international Christian ministry for the youth. I strive to model integrity, faith, and perseverance, showing how to embrace adversity.

Refer to the biblical verse James 1:2–5 as a prime example.

Above all, this book shows how some unfortunate situations can turn out to be blessings in disguise. This is a million-dollar benediction, food for thought—nourishing nutrients for the mind and soul that guide the body.

About the Author

Hosea Peterson was born and raised in Southeast Anacostia, Washington, DC. Once a product of his environment, Hosea grew from the trials and tribulations of his upbringing. He was introduced to his better half, his inner being—his "higher self"—and how that person put him on a broad path to greatness, providing an understanding of betterment for all who strive to apply both the law of the land and the secret law of attraction while bearing principles like integrity as he embarks on this newfound journey. His goal and purpose for publishing this book is to inspire people. Specifically, he wants to inspire them to do something they think they can't or want to do but are unaware of the infinite possibilities life has to offer. Hosea's encouraging persona enlightens others to embrace adversity and understand that it strengthens the spirit that dwells inside the body, guiding the mind and ultimately building character.

Since his youth, Hosea has had a love for cars. A car connoisseur, he makes it his mission to fix cars and restore them to a like-new condition. His passion for cars has led him to focus on something greater, with a higher purpose, and to avoid distractions. As readers delve into this memoir, he leaves them with this: "Let perseverance finish its work so that you may be mature and complete, not lacking anything. If you ask God, who gives generously to all without finding fault, it will be given to you. But when you ask, you must believe and not doubt, because the one who doubts is like a wave of the sea, blown and tossed by the wind."

He further shares, "It is said that success often results after hitting rock bottom or overcoming the biggest hurdle of the journey. Determination, patience, and courage are the only things needed to improve any situation. Adversity has the power to refocus your priorities, hone your character, unleash your most potent forces, and convert your struggle into fuel."

www.ingramcontent.com/pod-product-compliance
Lightning Source LLC
Chambersburg PA
CBHW020210120725
29413CB00032B/207
* 9 7 9 8 8 9 6 3 7 4 7 0 1 *